go! CHINESE 聽說讀打寫

Go 500

Textbook
(Traditional Character Edition)

IQChinese 策畫主編
Developed by IQChinese

CENGAGE
Learning®

Andover • Melbourne • Mexico City • Stamford, CT • Toronto • Hong Kong • New Delhi • Seoul • Singapore • Tokyo

Go! Chinese Go500 Textbook
(Traditional Character Edition)

Developed by IQChinese

Publishing Director:
Roy Lee

Editorial Manager, CLT:
Lan Zhao

Development Editor:
Coco Koh

Associate Development Editor:
Titus Teo

Creative Manager:
Melvin Chong

Senior Product Manager (Asia):
Joyce Tan

Product Manager (Outside Asia):
Mei Yun Loh

Regional Manager, Production & Rights:
Pauline Lim

Production Executive:
Cindy Chai / Evan Wu

Freelance Designer:
Jane Goh

ISBN-13: 978-981-4336-13-0
ISBN-10: 981-4336-13-0

Cengage Learning Asia Pte Ltd
151 Lorong Chuan
#02-08 New Tech Park
Singapore 556741

Cengage Learning is a leading provider of customized learning solutions with office locations around the globe, including Andover, Melbourne, Mexico City, Stamford (CT), Toronto, Hong Kong, New Delhi, Seoul, Singapore, and Tokyo. Locate your local office at **www.cengage.com/global**

Cengage Learning products are represented in Canada by Nelson Education, Ltd.

For product information, visit **www.cengageasia.com**

Photo Credits:
thinkstockphotos.com, Getty Images.

Printed in Taiwan
5 6 7 8 17 16 15 14

Acknowledgements

Go! Chinese is designed to be used together with *IQChinese Go* courseware, a series of multimedia CD-ROMs developed by *IQChinese*.

This series of textbooks, workbooks, and CD-ROMs would not have been possible without the contribution of the following experienced and dedicated individuals:

- **Mei-Hui Lee** (for contributing to the content of the CD-ROMs)
- **Hsiang-Yun Liang** (for contributing to the content of the CD-ROMs)
- **Julie Lo** (for advising on the pedagogy and curriculum)
- **Yi-Hua Tseng** (for contributing to the content of the books)
- **Hui-Chuan Wang** (for contributing to the content of the books and CD-ROMs)
- **Lanni Wang** (Instruction Specialist, IQChinese)
- **Meng-Tien Wu** (Instruction Manager, IQChinese)
- **Emily Yih** (for designing and planning the curriculum)
- **Ying-Xue Zhao** (for writing the reading texts which are age-appropriate and interesting)

We would also like to thank the following individuals who offered many helpful insights, ideas, and suggestions for improvement during the product development stage of *Go! Chinese*.

- **Jessie Lin Brown**, Singapore American School, Singapore
- **Deborah Chen**, Shammah Chinese School, USA
- **Henny Chen**, Moreau Catholic High School, USA
- **Yeafen Chen**, University of Wisconsin-Milwaukee, USA
- **Ting Ting Huang**, Grace Christian College, Philippines
- **Yi Liang Jiang**, Beijing Language and Culture University, China
- **Yan Jin**, Singapore American School, Singapore
- **Kerman Kwan**, Irvine Chinese School, USA
- **Andrew Scrimgeour**, University of South Australia, Australia
- **James L. Tan**, Grace Christian College, Philippines
- **Man Tao**, Koning Williem I College, the Netherlands
- **Chiungwen Tsai**, Westside Chinese School, USA
- **Tina Wu**, Westside High School, USA
- **YaWen (Alison) Yang**, Concordian international School, Thailand

Preface

Go! Chinese, together with *IQChinese Go* multimedia CD-ROM, is a fully-integrated Chinese language program that offers an easy, enjoyable, and effective learning experience for learners of Chinese as a foreign language.

The themes and lesson plans of this program are designed with references to the American National Standards for Foreign Language Learning developed by ACTFL[1], and the Curriculum Guides for Modern Languages developed by the Toronto District Board of Education. The program aims to help learners develop their communicative competence in the four language skills of listening, speaking, reading, and writing while gaining an appreciation of the Chinese culture. It allows learners to exercise their ability to compare and contrast different cultures, make connections with other discipline areas, and extend their learning experiences to their homes and communities.

The program employs innovative teaching methodologies and computer applications to enhance language learning, as well as keep students motivated in and outside of the classroom. The companion CD-ROM gives students access to audio, visual, and textual information about the language all at once. Chinese typing is systematically integrated into the program to facilitate the acquisition and retention of new vocabulary and to equip students with a skill that is becoming increasingly important in the Internet era wherein more and more professional and personal correspondence is done electronically.

Course Design

The program is divided into two series: Beginner and Intermediate. The Beginner Series, which comprises four levels (Go100-400), provides a solid foundation for continued study of the Intermediate Series (Go500-800). Each level includes a student text, a workbook, and a companion CD-ROM.

Beginner Series: Go100 – Go400

Designed for beginners, each level of the Beginner Series is made up of 10 colorfully illustrated lessons. Each lesson covers new vocabulary and simple sentence structures with particular emphasis on listening and speaking skills. In keeping with the communicative approach, a good mix of activities such as role play, interviews, games, pair work, and language exchanges are incorporated to allow students to learn to communicate through interaction in the target language. The CD-ROM uses rhythmic chants, word games, quizzes, and Chinese typing exercises to improve students' pronunciation, mastery of *pinyin*, and their ability to recognize and read words and sentences taught in each lesson.

The Beginner Series can be completed in roughly 240 hours (160 hours on Textbook and 80 hours on CD-ROM). Upon completion of the Beginner Series, the student will have acquired approximately 500 Chinese characters and 1000 common phrases.

Intermediate Series: Go500 – Go800

The Intermediate Series continues with the use of the communicative approach, but places a greater emphasis on Culture, Community, and Comparison. Through stories revolving around Chinese-American families, students learn vocabulary necessary for expressing themselves in a variety of contexts, describing their world, and discussing cultural differences.

The Intermediate Series can be completed in roughly 320 hours (240 hours on Textbook and 80 hours on CD-ROM). Upon completion of both the Beginner and Intermediate Series, the student will have acquired approximately 1000 Chinese characters and 2400 common phrases.

---

[1] American Council on the Teaching of Foreign Languages (http://www.actfl.org)

Vocabulary and Sentence Structures

The program places emphasis on helping students use the target language in contexts relevant to their everyday lives. Therefore, the chosen vocabulary and sentence structures are based on familiar topics such as family, school activities, hobbies, weather, shopping, food, pets, modes of transport, etc. The same topics are revisited throughout the series to reinforce learning, as well as to expand on the vocabulary and sentence structures acquired before.

Listening and Speaking

Communicative activities encourage and require a learner to speak with and listen to other learners. Well-designed and well-executed communicative activities can help turn the language classroom into an active and enjoyable place where learners are motivated to learn and can learn what they need. The program integrates a variety of communicative activities such as role play, interviews, games, pair work, and language exchanges to give students the opportunity to put what they have learned into practice.

Word Recognition and Reading

Each lesson introduces about 12 new Chinese characters. Using the spiral approach, each new character is first introduced and then repeated in classroom activities and subsequent lessons to enhance the retention of new vocabulary over time. From level Go500, instead of chants, students are exposed to passages which are approximately 500 words long. Through these reading passages, students are continually exposed to vocabulary, both old and new, and this also hones their reading skills. Exercises after the passages encourage critical thinking and discussion, stretching the students' comprehension skills and their capability to express themselves.

Pinyin (phonetic notation) is added above newly introduced characters so that students can learn to pronounce them. To make sure students do not become over-reliant on *pinyin* to read Chinese, recycled vocabulary is stripped of *pinyin* so that students can learn to recognize and read the actual written characters in due course. For the same reason, the CD-ROM companion does not display the *pinyin* of words automatically.

Culture

Cultural content is assimilated into each of the topics to allow students to get to know about different cultures. This also allows them to identify themselves in relation to the cultures introduced. Each volume also includes general knowledge components on the Chinese language to develop the students' understanding and appreciation of the language.

Type-to-Learn Methodology

The unique characteristic of this series is the use of Chinese typing as an instructional strategy to improve listening, pronunciation, and word recognition. Activities in the CD-ROM require students to type characters or sentences as they are read aloud or displayed on the computer screen. Students will be alerted if they make a mistake and will be given the chance to correct them. If they do not get it right on the third try, the software provides immediate feedback on how to correct the error. This interactive trial-and-error process allows students to develop self-confidence and learn the language by doing.

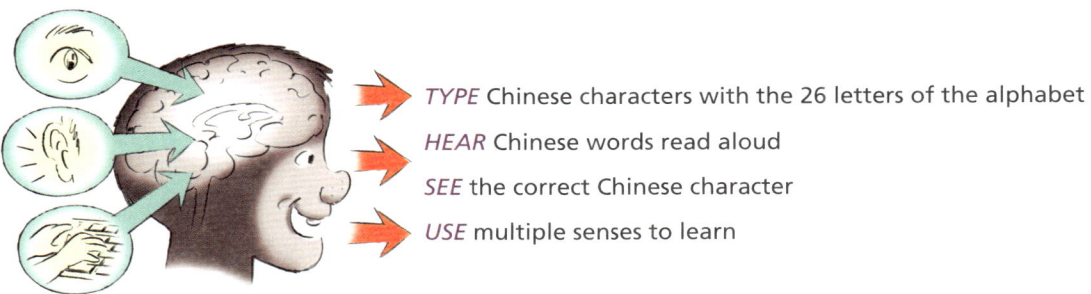

TYPE Chinese characters with the 26 letters of the alphabet

HEAR Chinese words read aloud

SEE the correct Chinese character

USE multiple senses to learn

Chinese Characters and Character Writing

The program does not require the student to be able to write all the core vocabulary; the teacher may however assign more character writing practice according to his or her classroom emphasis and needs. What the program aims to do is to give students a good grasp of Chinese radicals and stroke order rules, as well as to help students understand and appreciate the characteristics and formation of Chinese characters. The program includes writing practice on frequently used characters. Understanding the semantic function radicals have in the characters they form and having the ability to see compound characters by their simpler constituents enable students to memorize new characters in a logical way.

Using the CD-ROM as an Instructional Aid

The following diagram shows how a teacher might use the CD-ROM as an instructional aid to improve traditional classroom instruction.

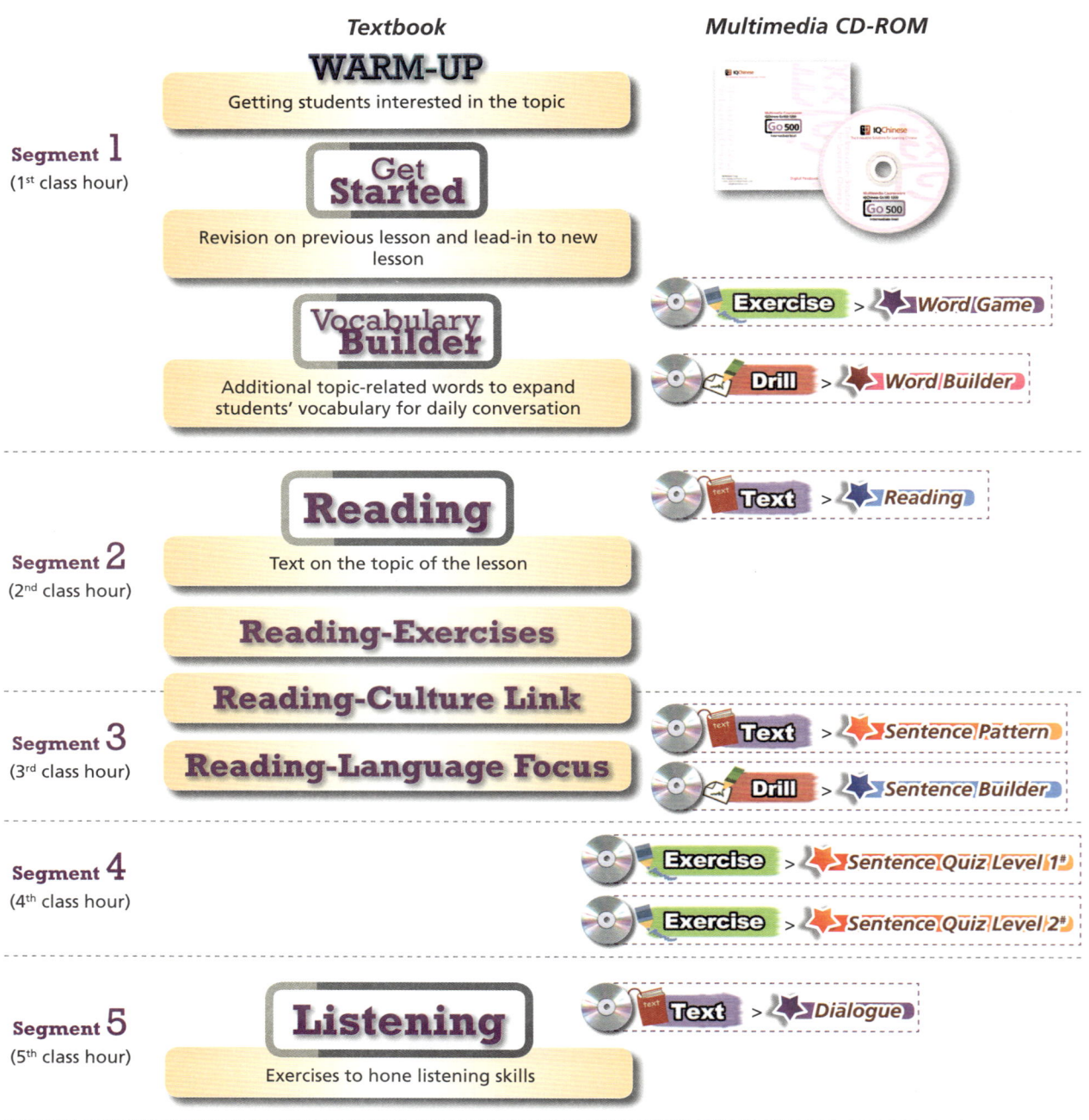

	Textbook	**Multimedia CD-ROM**

Segment 6
(6th class hour)

Listening-Language Focus

Listening-Culture Link

Segment 7
(7th class hour)

Role-Playing

Exercise > *Sentence Quiz Level 3#*

Exercise > *Sentence Quiz Level 4#*

Learn about the Chinese Language & Culture

Knowledge on the Chinese language and culture

Exercise > *Teacher's Assignment*

Segment 8
(8th class hour)

Work It Out

Review and reinforcement activities

LEARNING LOG

Conclusion and students' self-evaluation

 #Sentence Quiz Exercise

The section *Exercise > Sentence Quiz* on the CD-ROM enhances learning by stimulating multiple senses as well as providing immediate feedback on students' performance.

The Sentence Quiz exercise comprises four levels.

- Level 1 – Warm-up Quiz (Look, Listen, and Type): Chinese text, *pinyin*, and audio prompts are provided.
- Level 2 – Audio-aid Quiz: Only audio prompts are provided.
- Level 3 – Sentence Quiz: Reorder the words to form proper sentences.
- Level 4 – Comprehension Quiz: Type in the correct answers according to the content of the Reading and Dialogue components.

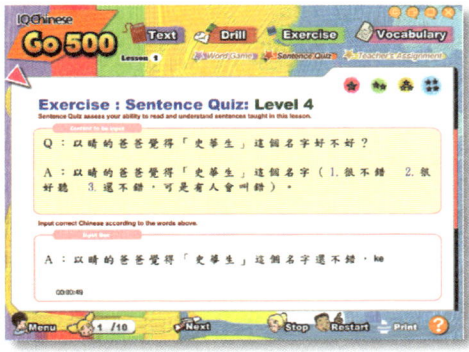

Type in the correct answer in the correct sequence, or according to the content of the text. This exercise tests the students' understanding of sentence patterns and comprehension skills.

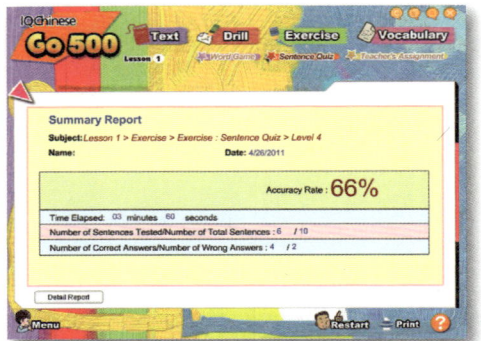

Summary report provides the percentage of correct answers given by the student, the total number of questions tried, and the total time spent on the exercise.

Detail report provides the correct answer to each question and a record of the student's answers.

Classroom Setup and Equipment

For small classes (up to 5 students), the teacher can show the CD-ROM features on one computer with students gathered around the screen. For large groups, a projector will be needed to project the computer's display onto a large screen so that the entire class can see.

If the classroom is not equipped with computers, the teacher may have students bring their own portable computers to class so that they can work individually or in small groups of 2 to 3 on the CD-ROM activities during designated class hours. CD-ROM activities may also be assigned as homework.

Suggestions for Teachers

We recommend that the teacher

- spend 6-7 hours on each lesson in the Textbook and 2 hours on each lesson on the CD-ROM. The course materials and lesson length may be adjusted according to students' proficiency level and learning ability.
- allocate 1-2 class hours to go over with the students the Review units in the Workbook as a way to check on their progress.
- have the students complete 1-2 pages of the Workbook after every two class sessions.
- encourage the students to spend 10 minutes a day on the Sentence Quiz in the CD-ROM. Practice makes perfect!

More Support

IQChinese is the publisher for **IQChinese Go** multimedia CD-ROMs. By adopting Type-To-Learn as its core methodology, IQChinese provides learners of the Chinese language a complete solution to learn the language effectively.

Courseware & Homework

IQChinese offers additional resources for both teachers and students:

eClass (http://eclass.iqchinese.com): offers additional lesson-by-lesson practices, and allows teachers to create own assignments and quizzes.

IQChinese Fun (http://www.iqchinesefun.com): visit the website or use mobile applications for iPhone, iPad, and iPod Touch to learn and practice Chinese characters in a fun and interesting way.

- "Type-to-Learn" courseware for PC & Mac
- textbook & workbook
- online practice system
- mobile practice apps for iOS
- Chinese learning software

Teaching Support

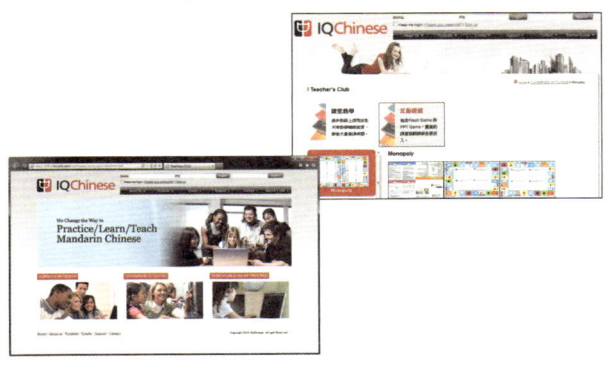

Online teacher workshops, additional classroom activities and resources such as detailed chapter-by-chapter lesson plans, teaching slides, and supplementary assignments are developed to facilitate classroom teaching. Visit the following websites for more information.

Cengage Learning http://www.cengageasia.com

IQChinese Teacher's Club http://www.iqchinese.com

- online teaching resources
- teacher training & workshops
- supporting software

Technical Support

IQChinese offers technical support for product installation, school site licensing, digital lesson planning, etc. If you require technical assistance, please contact iqservice@iqchinese.com

- product installation
- school site license
- digital learning conversion
- digital teaching planning

Scope & Sequence

Words marked with an asterisk (*) are supplementary vocabulary.

Lesson	Communicative Goals	Vocabulary	Language Focus	Cultural Information
我的名字 My Name **1**	• Introduce myself in Chinese • Describe the actions, ways or processes taken to fulfill an intention • Use "你覺得……最好？" to seek others' opinions	**Self-introduction and origins of names** 家人, 華人, 像, 死, 記/記住, 美國人, 取(名字), 那樣, 讓, 覺得, 花生, 為了, 如果, 最後, 介紹, 哭, 意思, 妳 *兄弟, 孩子, 姐妹, 華文, 不像, 生, 忘記, 漂亮, 品德, 順利, 富貴, 成功, 平安, 聰明, 美好, 文靜	• "有人……，也有人……" 有人叫他們Bill和Cindy，也有人叫他們華生和心如。 • "為了……" 為了給我取名字，爸爸和媽媽吵了很久。 • "你覺得……最好？" 你覺得怎麼介紹自己最好？	• How the Chinese name their children • How the Chinese introduce their surnames • The evolution of Chinese characters
我的同學 My Classmates **2**	• Introduce my classmates by talking about our shared interests and their countries of origin • Pinpoint a starting time from which an event or situation occurs • Use "……的時候，……" to offer a solution to a problem	**Names of countries and introduction of my classmates** 美國, 英國, 日本, 臺灣, 中國, 印度, 年級, 中學生, 原來, 小學, 不過, 運氣, 讀書, 長大, 懂, 阿, 男生, 英國人, 日文, 出生, 中學, 初中 *加拿大, 墨西哥, 巴西, 智利, 西班牙, 法國, 德國, 義大利, 香港, 澳大利亞, 紐西蘭, 沙烏地阿拉伯, 埃及, 南非	• "從……起，……" 從今年九月起，我就是七年級的學生。 • "……的時候，……" 他們聽不懂英文的時候，我可以幫他們忙。	• The unique cultures of different countries • Writing direction of Chinese texts and sentences
我的朋友 My Friends **3**	• Introduce my friends • Indicate that an event only occurs during a stated time • Describe an action meted to another and the underlying intention • Use reduplication of measure word to describe a situation where there is no exception	**Description of personalities** 女孩, 外向, 內向, 說話, 交朋友, 一些, 中華, 文化, 餐館, 越南人, 洗衣店, 其他, 跟, 以後, 老先生, 越南 *性別, 男性, 男孩, 女性, 個性, 幽默, 溫和, 體貼, 自信, 被動, 主動, 大方, 活潑, 害羞, 好客, 開朗, 溫柔, 負責, 樂觀, 獨立, 誠實	• "從……到……，只有……(才)……" 從早忙到晚，只有星期日(才)休息。 • "(subject) 把……讓……" 他們把圓圓送來我家，讓我照顧她。 • "(Reduplication of measure words) 都……" (我)天天都要找朋友說話。	• The meaning of 忘年之交 • The culture of using seals in Chinese history

Lesson	Communicative Goals	Vocabulary	Language Focus	Cultural Information
我愛看的書 My Favorite Books 4	• Recommend a book proficiently in Chinese • Use "越來越……" to express the increasing intensity of a matter • Convey that somebody is asking someone else to perform a task	**Genres of books and ways to talk about books** 詩, 小說, 故事書, 小時候, 念, 十萬, 這些, 而且, 壞人, 故事, 可怕, 越, 像, 好像, 棒, 裡面, 卻 *神話, 童話, 寓言, 科普書, 圖畫書, 漫畫書, 雜誌, 推理, 恐怖, 奇幻, 愛情, 武俠, 歷史, 書名, 作者, 繪者, 翻譯/譯者, 出版社	• "……而且……" 小說字太多了，而且有些小說故事很可怕，讓人很緊張。 • "越來越……" 我越來越喜歡看小說了。 • "要……把……" 媽媽要我把中文學好。 • "可以……，也可以……" 我可以寫得長，也可以寫得短。	• Chinese stories: Journey to the West (西遊記), Mulan Serving in the Army for Father (木蘭代父從軍), The Three Kingdoms (三國演義) • Chinese verse: 5-character quatrain (五言絕句), limericks (打油詩)
我們去買菜 Let's Go to the Market 5	• Talk about my experience at the market • Convey a consequence that one is afraid of or unwilling to suffer • Use multiple adjectives to state the qualities of an item	**Food and taste** 蛋, 皮蛋, 豆腐, 麻婆豆腐, 阿姨, 於是, 千, 搖頭/搖搖頭, 敢, 怕, 龍眼, 水果, 龍, 啊, 有名, 頭 *蛋花湯, 豆子, 酸, 甜, 苦, 辣, 鹹, 油, 醬油, 醋, 胡椒粉, 鹽, 糖, 辣椒, 大蒜, 蔥	• "(subject) 怕……" 他怕吃了龍的眼睛，龍會生氣。 • "什麼……又 (adjective) 又 (adjective)？" 什麼中國菜又好吃又容易做？	• The origin of Mapo Tofu • Different culinary habits between Chinese and Westerners • Recognize pictographic characters and ideograms
誰來做家事？ Who Does the Housework? 6	• Talk about the household chores I can do • Describe the condition that needs to be satisfied before a proposition is allowed • Use questions to negate a proposition • Highlight the fact that a situation is different from the norm	**Names of household chores** 整理, 家事, 呢, 變, 收, 歡迎, 一定, 小孩, 當然, 院子, 男孩/男孩子, 雖然, 但是 *擦窗戶, 洗窗簾, 刷馬桶, 洗浴缸, 鋪床, 拖地, 掃地, 吸地, 整理廚房, 擦流理台, 倒垃圾, 擦乾碗盤, 收拾碗盤, 摺衣服, 燙衣服, 遛狗, 澆花, 曬衣服	• "怎麼可以……呢？" 怎麼可以叫客人做家事呢？ • "把……，才可以……" 把東西收好，才可以回家。 • "雖然……，但是……" 以思雖然小，但是他洗碗洗得很乾淨。	• Social expectations of a Chinese host and his guest • Traditional gender roles (males as breadwinners and females as homemakers)
廚房安全 Safety in the Kitchen 7	• Identify household risks and suggest ways to make the home safer • Make suggestions tactfully and less forceful • Rebut a proposition using a negative question	**Kitchen appliances, ways of cooking, and safety in the kitchen** 關火, 日子, 己經, 節, 吧, 火, 熱水, 離開, 檢查 *電鍋, 水壺, 鍋子, 水龍頭, 瓦斯爐, 微波爐, 烤箱, 冰箱, 菜刀, 切菜板, 開火, 加熱, 煎, 煮, 蒸, 燉, 炒, 炸, 烤, 危險, 受傷, 滑倒, 燙傷, 切, 倒(水), 觸電, 失火	• "……已經……了" 以思已經十歲了。 • "讓……吧！" 讓我們幫以思上第一節課吧！ • "……的時候，(我)不是……嗎？" 我洗菜的時候，(我)不是在洗手嗎？	• The traditional view that males do not work in the kitchen • Recognize picto-phonetic characters and associative compound characters

Lesson	Communicative Goals	Vocabulary	Language Focus	Cultural Information
我的學校 My School **8**	• Introduce my school and my community • Describe the different aspects of a particular scenario • Convey a reason and a corresponding result • Use contrasting concepts to highlight something	**My school life and the environment of my school** 校園, 參觀, 貼, 留話, 櫃子, 排隊, ……排, 願意, 午飯, 鞋子, 吉, 商店, 大門, 大吉大利, 倒/倒過來, 舊 *環境, 走廊, 聊天, 校車, 幫助, 選課, 分組, 做實驗, 小組討論	• "……，這樣……才……" 學校小、學生少，這樣，老師才能認識每一個學生。 • "……，有的……，有的……，還有……" 櫃子的門上有很多留話，有的是用英文寫的，有的是用日文寫的，還有一句用中文寫的。 • "雖然……，可是……" 雖然很忙，可是很開心。	• How the Chinese usher in good luck and fortune • Recognize Chinese Spring couplets
中國新年 Lunar New Year **9**	• Describe the traditions observed during the Lunar New Year and their origins • Use reduplication of adjectives in the form of AABB • State the similarity between two concepts	**Lunar New Year greetings and customs** 恭喜, 發財, 餘, 平安, 年糕, 水餃, 紅包, 新年, 年夜飯, 過年, 吉利話, 留, 甜, 聲音, 塊, 壓歲錢, 發, 大人, 壓/壓著 *萬事如意, 恭賀新禧, 心想事成, 年年有餘, 步步高升, 歲歲平安, 吉祥如意, 招財進寶, 財源滾滾, 開張大吉, 長命百歲, 金榜題名, 一帆風順, 發糕, 橘子, 春聯, 鞭炮	• "健健康康" (Reduplication of adjectives) 媽媽希望孩子健健康康的。 媽媽希望孩子健健康康地長大。 • "……跟……一樣，都……" 日本新年跟美國新年一樣，都是一月一日。	• How the Chinese celebrate Lunar New Year • The significance of eating dumplings during the Lunar New Year • The origin of 壓歲錢 (money given to children during the Lunar New Year) • Recognize pairs of Chinese couplets
有趣的中國字 Interesting Chinese Characters **10**	• Use mnemonics to remember Chinese characters • Convey the sudden realization of a fact • Express my personal opinion or offer a suggestion	**Chinese radicals and opposites** 聰明, 清楚, 奇怪, 可憐, 安心, 方塊, 吵, 女人, 腦, 應該, 站, 爭吵, 發現, 青/青色 *竹, 言, 木, 目, 糸, 食, 广, 宀, 疒, 辵, 模糊, 笨, 常, 煩惱	• "……原來……啊！" 孫以安原來是一個女生啊！ • "我覺得……最好！" 我覺得以思的名字應該叫「孫以忘」最好！	• Radicals in Chinese characters • Revision on the formation of Chinese characters

Table of Contents

我的名字
My Name

1 What are they doing?

2 If it were you, how would you introduce yourself?

My Goals

1 Introduce myself in Chinese

2 Understand the cultural significance of choosing a Chinese name

3 Describe the actions, ways, or processes taken to fulfill an intention

4 Seek others' opinions in Chinese

5 Become familiar with vocabulary commonly used to introduce oneself

A

Based on the given scenario, number the following texts in the correct order.

SCENARIO: It is Sunny's (以晴) first day at school tomorrow. At 11:30pm, Sunny's mother finds that she still has not gone to bed…

1 以晴，怎麼還不睡覺？明天第一天上課，別太晚睡。

□ *妳可以說妳的名字、愛好、喜歡的學科，大家就能更快認識妳。

□ 沒關係，只要多參加活動，就能認識新朋友了。

□ 媽媽，我有一點兒緊張。到了新學校，我一個朋友也不認識。

□ 參加活動的時候，我要和新朋友、新同學說什麼？

□ 我知道了，謝謝媽媽！

*妳 you (female)

B

In pairs, take on the roles of Mother and Sunny respectively and read aloud the dialogue in the correct order. Exchange roles and repeat the exercise.

Vocabulary Builder

jiā rén 家人	xiōng dì 兄弟 (brothers)	huá rén 華人 华
hái zi 孩子 (children)	jiě mèi 姊妹 (sisters) 姐	huá wén 華文 (Chinese language) 华

xiàng 像		sǐ 死	jì jì zhù 记 记 記/記住
⇕	⇕	⇕	⇕
bú xiàng 不像 (different)	shēng 難 难 生 (born)		wàng jì 忘記記 (forget)

容易

piào liàng 漂亮 (pretty)	pǐn dé 品德 (moral character)	shùn lì 顺順利 (smooth-sailing)
fù guì 富貴贵 (rich and influential)	chéng gōng 成功 (successful)	píng ān 平安 (safe)
cōng míng 聰明 聪 (smart)	měi hǎo 美好 (fine)	wén jìng 文靜靜 (gentle and quiet)

New Words

jiā rén 家人	family
huá rén 華人 华	Chinese (people)
xiàng 像	like; alike
sǐ 死	die
jì jì zhù 記/記住	remember

Guess the Words

1 Stand in lines of 4 to 6 people. Send the last person in each line to the teacher for a word.

2 Without any verbal communication, the aforementioned team member is to return to his position in the line and write the *pinyin* of that word on the back of his team mate for the latter to guess the word. The word is to be passed down the line in this fashion.

3 Once the word is conveyed to the first person in the row, he is to take the placard that carries the word from the board and read it aloud to win the round.

我的名字 3

SCENARIO: Want to get to know Sunny more? In the following text, Sunny introduces herself and her family.

我的中文名字叫「孫以晴」，英文名字叫 Sunny Mary Swanson。我爸爸是美國人，媽媽是華人。我的英文名字是爸爸取的，爸爸希望我像陽光一樣，人人都喜歡。我的中文名字是媽媽取的，她希望我天天都像「晴天」那樣，讓人開心，讓人喜歡。

我爸爸叫 William Swanson。他學中文的時候，老師給他取了一個中文名字，叫「史華生」。他覺得這個中文名字還不錯，可是，有的人中文說得不好，常常叫他「死花生」。媽媽叫「孫心如」，英文名字是 Cindy Sun。❶有人叫他們 Bill 和 Cindy，也有人叫他們「華生」和「心如」。

❷為了給我取名字，爸爸和媽媽吵了很久。爸爸希望我的中文名字叫「史美麗」。他說，Mary 是奶奶的名字，Mary 和中文的「美麗」很像，他也希望我「美麗」。可是，媽媽不喜歡。她說，第一，叫

「美麗」的人太多；第二，華人(huá rén)不喜歡家人(jiā rén)取(qǔ)一樣的名字；第三，如果(rú guǒ)英文名字用爸爸的姓——Swanson，那麼中文名字就得用媽媽的姓——孫。

最後(zuì hòu)，媽媽讓(ràng)爸爸給我們取(qǔ)英文名字，爸爸讓(ràng)媽媽給我們取(qǔ)中文名字，我們一家五個人的名字就是：

爸爸	：	史華(huá)生 (William Swanson)
媽媽	：	孫心如(rú) (Cindy Swanson)
哥哥	：	孫以安 (Ian William Swanson)
我	：	孫以晴 (Sunny Mary Swanson)
弟弟	：	孫以思 (Ethan John Swanson)

New Words

měi guó rén 美國人	American	
qǔ 取(名字)	give a name	
nà yàng 那樣	in that way	
ràng 讓	allow; give way to	
jué de 覺得	feel; think	
huā shēng 花生	peanut	
wèi le 為了	in order to; because of	
rú guǒ 如果	if	
zuì hòu 最後	finally	

Exercises

True or False?

Answer the questions according to the passage.

對　錯

1. 以晴的爸爸叫「史華生」，他是華人。　　○　　⊘

2. 以晴的媽媽不希望孩子的名字和奶奶一樣。　⊘　　○

3. 有的人不喜歡以晴的爸爸，所以叫他「死花生」。　○　　⊘

4. 以晴的爸爸的中文名字和英文名字聽起來有一點兒像。　⊘　　○

5. 美國人常給孩子取跟家人一樣的名字。　⊘　　○

Think & Discuss

Work in pairs and answer the questions in Chinese.

1. 以晴的爸爸、媽媽想給以晴取的中文名字有什麼不一樣？你喜歡哪一個？

2. 以晴的哥哥叫 Ian William Swanson，這個名字是爸爸還是媽媽取的？你是怎麼知道的？

Culture Link

The Chinese believe that one's name can determine his destiny. Hence, much thought is put into giving names. A Chinese name can reveal much information about a person, such as the hopes and wishes his elders have for him, his time of birth, the season when he was born, or his birth order in his family.

At times, siblings may share a common character in their names, to signify that they belong to a particular generation in that family. For example, 以安, 以晴, and 以思 share a common character (以) to signify that they belong to the same generation. Unlike Western cultures, where many individuals are named after their elders, it is a taboo in Chinese culture for one to be named after an elder. In some cases, even phonetically-similar names are avoided.

Do you have a Chinese name? Who named you and what is the meaning behind your name? If you do not have a Chinese name, ask your teacher or someone well-versed in Chinese to give you one.

1

有人　叫他們 Bill 和 Cindy，

帶小狗去公園跑步，

也有人　叫他們華生(huá shēng)和心如(xīn rú)。

帶孩子(hái zi)去公園散步。

> **TIP** When 有 is followed by 人, the two characters function as a semantic unit meaning "some of the people". The phrase "有人……，也有人……" provides a list of the behavior, actions, or attitudes of some people in a location.

A: 大家去公園做什麼？

B: 有人去公園休息，也有人去公園運動。

A: 你們怎麼學中文？

B: 有人看書學中文，也有人用電腦學中文。

 **PRACTICE IT** Using sentence structure 1, complete the dialogues with the helping words and phrases.

1. A: 你們怎麼去學校？

   B: 有人_____去，也有人_____去。

2. A: 大家在餐廳做什麼？

   B: 有人在餐廳_____，也有人在餐廳

   _____。

3. A: 大家送你什麼生日禮物？

   B: 有人送我_____，也有人送我_____。

走路
吃飯
筆
喝咖啡
坐公車
書

2 為了 wèi le	給我取名字， qǔ	爸爸和媽媽吵了很久。
	認識新朋友，	我參加了很多活動。

A: 你為什麼每天都很晚才睡覺？

B: 為了看晚上十點半的節目，
wèi le
我每天都很晚才睡覺。

A: 你星期六還要上課嗎？

B: 對！為了學中文，我每個星期
wèi le
六都到學校上課。

PRACTICE IT

Using sentence structure 2, complete the dialogues with the helping phrases.

> **TIP**
> The phrase containing 為了 conveys a motive or intention. The clause that follows it conveys the way or the process taken to fulfill the intention. In the first example, 為了給我取名字，爸爸和媽媽吵了很久, the intention was to choose a name for the narrator and in the process, his parents argued for a long time.

1. A: 謝小明為什麼去圖書館？

   B: _____

   _____

2. A: 你喜歡運動嗎？

   B: 不喜歡，可是_____

   _____

3. A: 你為什麼要學中文？

   B: _____

   _____

Group A

和只會講中文
的奶奶講電話

寫作業

身體健康

Group B

學中文

每天跑步

去圖書館找書

Go 500 **WANT TO LEARN MORE?**

Check out the Text > Sentence Pattern section on the Go500 CD.

Listening

Go500

Text > Dialogue section

SCENARIO: During a lesson, the teacher asks that every student speaks on stage.

A Listen to the Go500 CD for the dialogue and answer the following multiple-choice questions.

1. 老師要以晴做什麼？ *A*

　　jiè shào　　　　jiè shào　　　　jiè shào
(A) 介紹自己　(B) 介紹同學　(C) 介紹學校

2. 以晴覺得她的中文名字怎麼樣？ *C*
　　jué de

(A) 好看　(B) 容易寫　(C) 好聽

3. 媽媽為什麼給以晴取這個名字？  *C*
　　　　　　　　　　　　　qǔ

(A) 希望不要常常下雨。　　(B) 希望她不要常常哭。
　　　　　　　　　　　　　　　　　　　　　　　　　kū

(C) 希望大家天天想到她。

4. 以晴覺得怎樣介紹自己最好？ *B*
　　　jué de　　　jiè shào

(A) 先讓大家看到你。
　　ràng
(B) 讓大家容易記住你的名字。
　　ràng　　　　　jì zhù
(C) 要笑著介紹自己的名字。
　　　　　　jiè shào

5. 下面哪一個對？ *C*

(A) 以晴的中文名字有常常下雨的意思。
　　　　　　　　　　　　　　　　　　　yì si
(B) 以晴覺得媽媽給她取錯中文名字了。
　　　　jué de　　　　qǔ
(C) 以晴的中文名字和英文名字很像。
　　　　　　　　　　　　　　　　xiàng

New Words

jiè shào 介紹	introduce
kū 哭	cry
yì si 意思	meaning
nǐ 妳	you (feminine)

B Number the following texts in the correct order to form a coherent conversation.

☐ 老師：以晴，妳的中文名字＿＿＿＿＿＿，是誰給妳取的？

以晴：我的中文名字是＿＿＿＿＿＿＿＿＿。我小的時候
很愛哭，媽媽希望我像晴天，不要常常下雨。

☐ 老師：❸妳覺得怎麼介紹自己最好？

以晴：介紹自己的時候，第一，先讓大家知道＿＿＿＿
＿＿＿；第二，要讓大家＿＿＿＿就能記住你的
名字。

1 老師：請妳介紹妳自己讓大家認識。

以晴：大家好！我是孫以晴。「以」是「＿＿＿＿＿」
的「以」，「晴」是「＿＿＿＿＿」的「晴」。
晴天時，大家會想到我；陰天時，大家更會
想看到我。謝謝大家。

3 老師：妳喜歡這個名字嗎？

以晴：我覺得還不錯。因為
我的＿＿＿＿＿＿和
＿＿＿＿＿＿很像，
好聽又容易記。

C Listen to the conversation on the Go500 CD again, and fill in the blanks.

3 妳覺得 ^{nǐ jué de} | 怎麼介紹自己 ^{jiè shào}
買什麼給他 | 最好？

A: 籃球比賽從星期六到下個星期一都可以參加，你覺得 ^{jué de} 我們什麼時候去最好？

B: 我覺得 ^{jué de} 星期六下午去最好。

A: 以思還沒有回教室，你覺得 ^{jué de} 我們怎麼做最好？

B: 我們最好先和老師說！

> **TIP**
> A speaker may use "你覺得 ⋯⋯最好？" to ask for others' opinions. Between 覺得 and 最好, an interrogative phrase such as 誰, 怎麼, 什麼, 哪裡, 多少, 幾點 is used, depending on the content of the question. In reply, it is not necessary to answer using the same sentence structure; one can simply state his opinion.

PRACTICE IT

Complete the dialogues using sentence structure 3.

1. A: 你覺得 ^{jué de} _____ 最好？

   B: 我覺得 ^{jué de} 我們在家吃飯最好。

2. A: 你覺得 ^{jué de} _____ 最好？

   B: 爸爸喜歡運動，我想送運動鞋給他。

3. A: 小明的生日會和哥哥的球賽在同一天，你覺得 ^{jué de}

   _____ 最好？

   B: 我們可以早上先去看球賽，下午再去小明的生日會。

Go500 💿 **WANT TO LEARN MORE?**

Check out the Text > Sentence Pattern section on the Go500 CD.

Culture Link

As the Chinese language is made up of many homophones, it is common for one to break down his surname into its components when introducing himself, for example, "耳 (the radical in *陳)東，陳", "*弓長，*張", and "雙 *木，*林". Sometimes, commonly-used phrases are used to introduce one's name. For example, a name like *李春日 may be introduced as木子 李, 春 as in 春天, and 日 as in 生日. Nonetheless, one should take care to avoid negative phrases when introducing his name.

chén zhāng lín lǐ   gōng mù

*陳，張，林，李 Chinese surnames 弓 bow 木 wood

TALK ABOUT IT

In pairs, discuss how you would introduce the following names.

1. 李愛美：_____

2. 林慶安：_____

3. _____ (your Chinese name)：_____

Role Playing

Form groups of four and role-play the scenario. You may use the sentence structures provided below.

CHARACTERS:

媽媽, 以思, 以晴, 以安

SCENARIO:

After school, 以晴 recounts to her family how she introduced herself to others in school. 以安 and 以思 find the experience rather meaningful, and have a go at introducing themselves.

SENTENCE STRUCTURES:

1. 有人……，也有人……

2. 為了……
   wèi le

3. 只要……就……

4. 你覺得……最好？
   jué de

5. 是(誰)……的？

Learn about the Chinese Language & Culture

你知道嗎？中國文字有三千多年的歷史了。

「我」這是我，「𢦏」這是我，「𢎾」這還是我，「𢦒」這也是我。從以前到現在，文字的樣子長得不太一樣。

下面這些都是你認識的字，不過你學的是文字現在的樣子。你能認出這幾個文字以前的樣子嗎？

Name of Script	甲骨文 jiǎ gǔ wén (Oracle Bone Script)	金文 jīn wén (Bronze Script)	小篆 xiǎo zuàn (Small Seal Script)	楷體/正體字 kǎi tǐ zhèng tǐ zì (Standard Script)	簡體字 jiǎn tǐ zì (Simplified Script)
Period	1400-1200BC	1046-256BC	221BC-8AD	25BC-now	1956AD-now
Carved or written on ...	骨頭、石頭 gǔ tou shí tou (bone, stone)	銅器 tóng qì (copper)	竹片 zhú piàn (bamboo slates)	紙	紙

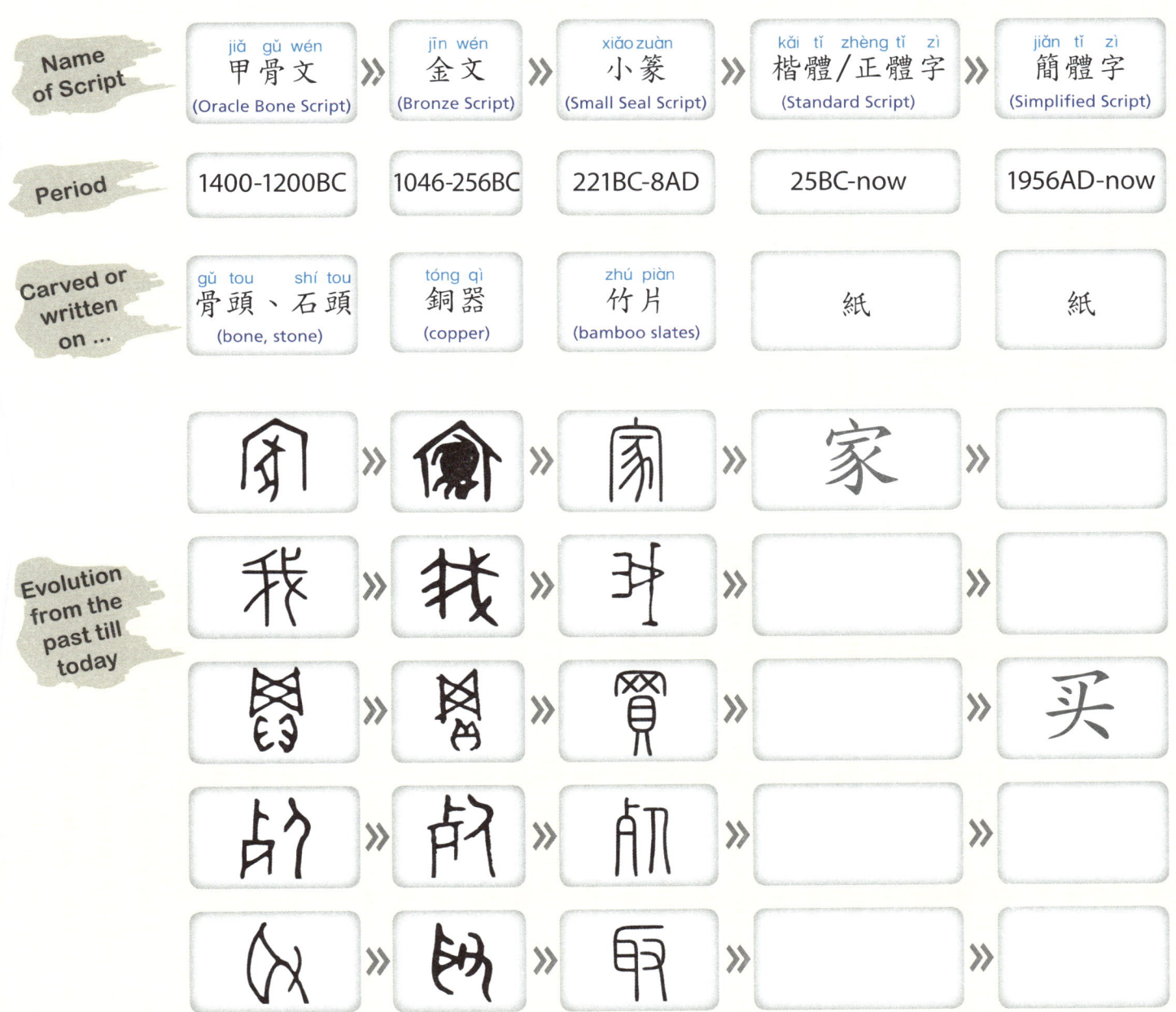

Evolution from the past till today

Work It Out

Introducing ourselves in a memorable and interesting manner not only breaks the ice between strangers, it also leaves a good and lasting impression on others quickly.

TASK

Introduce Your Friends

1 Form groups of four. Take turns to introduce your names and interests, following the way Sunny introduces herself on page 10.

2 Fill in the table below with your teammates' introductions.

3 Introduce these three friends of yours to another three friends.

	Chinese Name	Introduction
1.		
2.		
3.		

LEARNING LOG

I can...

		Excellent	Good	Fair	Need Improvement
1	introduce myself by stating my name in a way that is memorable to others.	○	○	○	○
2	state the cultural differences in the way the Chinese and Americans choose their names.	○	○	○	○
3	use the structures "有人……，也有人……" and "為了……" to form sentences.	○	○	○	○
4	use the structure "你覺得……最好？" to seek others' opinions.	○	○	○	○
5	write 介紹, 最後, 記住, and 意思.	○	○	○	○

我的同學
My Classmates

1 Do you have friends who are foreigners? Which countries do they come from?

2 Why is it interesting to be with these friends?

My Goals

1 Introduce my classmates in Chinese
2 Pinpoint a starting time from which an event or situation occurs
3 Offer solutions to specific problems or difficulties
4 Recognize the direction in which Chinese texts and sentences are written
5 Become familiar with names of various countries

A Based on the pictures, complete the following sentences using the helping phrases.

我叫謝小明，我有兩個好朋友。我們

每天＿＿＿＿＿＿＿＿＿＿＿＿＿＿。

（一起……，一起……）

我們＿＿＿＿＿＿＿＿＿＿＿＿＿＿

＿＿＿＿＿＿＿＿＿＿＿＿＿＿＿。

（只要……，就……）

我們三個人＿＿＿＿＿＿＿＿＿＿＿

＿＿＿＿＿＿＿＿＿＿＿＿＿＿＿。

（有人……，也有人……）

B Read your completed sentences aloud to your classmates.

Vocabulary Builder

jiā ná dà
加拿大
(Canada)

yīng guó
英國

rì běn
日本

ào dà lì yà
澳大利亞
(Australia)

měi guó
美國

xī bān yá
西班牙
(Spain)

zhōng guó
中國

niǔ xī lán
紐西蘭
(New Zealand)

mò xī gē
墨西哥
(Mexico)

fǎ guó
法國
(France)

tái wān
臺灣

shā wū dì ā lā bó
沙烏地阿拉伯
(Saudi Arabia)

bā xī
巴西
(Brazil)

dé guó
德國
(Germany)

xiāng gǎng
香港
(Hong Kong)

āi jí
埃及
(Egypt)

zhì lì
智利
(Chile)

yì dà lì
義大利
(Italy)

yìn dù
印度
(India)

nán fēi
南非
(South Africa)

Guess the Countries

1 Get ready a map and get into small teams.

2 Each team sends a representative in front to select a country.

3 The rest of the teams take turns to guess the country their representative has selected.

4 The representative can only state "too far" or "too close" in reply to indicate the distance between the chosen country and the country given by the teams.

5 The team which guesses the correct country first wins.

New Words

měi guó 美國	the U.S.	yīng guó 英國	the U.K.
rì běn 日本	Japan	tái wān 臺灣	Taiwan
zhōng guó 中國	China	yìn dù 印度	India

SCENARIO: From September, 孫以晴 will be starting seventh grade in a new school. With this change, she realizes that everything will be very different …

我今年十二歲，❶從今年九月起，我就是七年級的學生，也是中學生，要去新學校上課。在原來的小學裡，校長、老師和同學我都認識，教室在哪裡我也知道。現在的新學校比原來的學校大，老師和同學也比原來的學校多；開學的時候，我很緊張，常常找不到教室。不過，我的運氣好，我的好朋友們也都來這個新學校讀書。

我有四個好朋友。久美子的爸媽從日本來，她和我一起長大，她比我小四個月。張靜從中國來，她來美國兩年了，還在上*ESL的課。❷她聽不懂英文的時候，我會幫她的忙。阿明是男生，他和家人從印度來，他的數學和電腦都很好，我們常常問他問題。安地的爸爸是英國人，媽媽是美國人。他喜歡和我們在一起，因為他想學中文和日文。可是，到現在，他只會說「謝謝」和「O-Ha-Yo」。

*ESL: English as a Second Language

我們五個人在學校裡一起上課，一起參加活動；下課後，我們常常一起做功課、看電影和打球。同學都叫我們High Five。

New Words

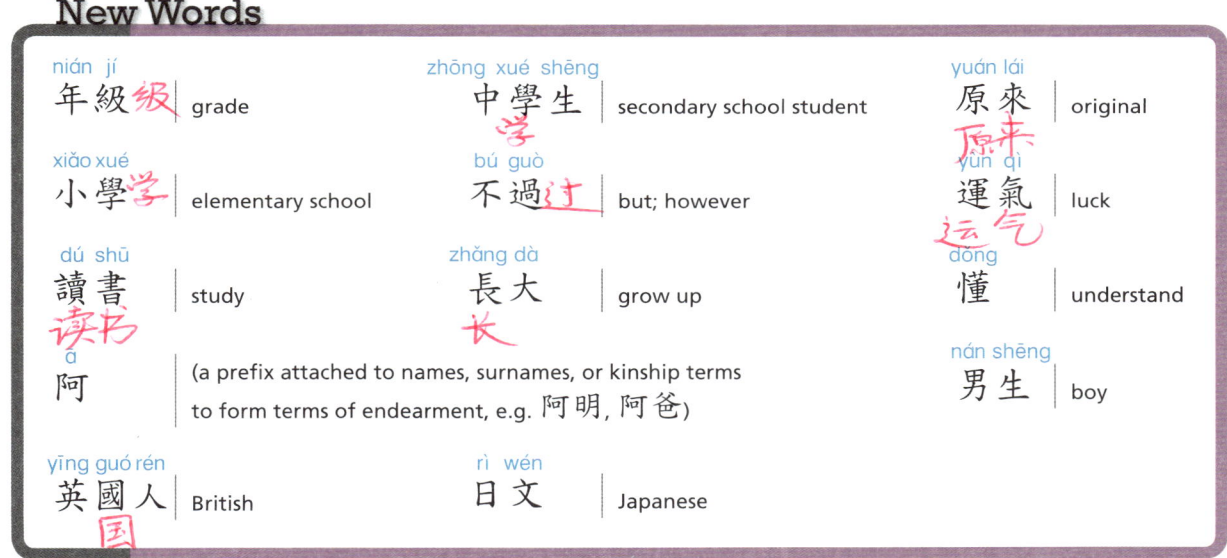

nián jí 年级	grade	zhōng xué shēng 中學生	secondary school student	yuán lái 原來	original
xiǎo xué 小學	elementary school	bú guò 不過	but; however	yùn qì 運氣	luck
dú shū 讀書	study	zhǎng dà 長大	grow up	dǒng 懂	understand
a 阿	(a prefix attached to names, surnames, or kinship terms to form terms of endearment, e.g. 阿明, 阿爸)			nán shēng 男生	boy
yīng guó rén 英國人	British	rì wén 日文	Japanese		

Exercises

Answer the questions according to the passage.

		對	錯
1. 新學校的老師和同學，以晴一個都不認識。		○	⊘
2. 以晴比久美子小。		○	⊘
3. 以晴的英文比張靜好。		⊘	○
4. 安地不用上ESL的課。		⊘	○
5. 安地的中文和日文(rì wén)都說得不錯。		○	⊘

Fill It In

Complete the table by filling in the details on 以晴 and her friends, as gathered from the passage above. Write "－" in the box if no information is available.

	以晴	久美子	張靜	阿明	安地
Gender	女生				男生
Father's nationality	美國人				
Mother's nationality	華人				

Think & Discuss

Work in pairs and answer the questions in Chinese.

1. 以晴的新學校和原來(yuán lái)的學校有什麼不一樣？

2. 張靜什麼時候需要以晴的幫忙？你最常幫同學什麼忙？

3. 你有哪些好朋友？你們常常在一起做什麼？

Culture Link

Every country has its unique culture. Japan brings to mind traditional costumes such as the kimono, as well as delectable and healthy sushi. The thought of China evokes images of Chinese cuisine with its tantalizing combination of presentation, aroma, and taste. One may associate India with its religious mystique as well as the people's way of life there. Such are cultures across the globe that make our world so interesting.

TALK ABOUT IT

With a partner, identify the countries that are associated with the following pictures.

(carnival)

(Beijing opera)

(spices)

(traditional Scottish costumes)

(bull-fighting)

Besides these pictures, can you name more cultural features of these countries?

(Chinese cuisine)

(hula dancing)

(sushi)

		今年九月		我就是七年級的學生。
1	從		起，	
		明天		我要每天坐公車去上學。

A: 你要去英國讀書了？

B: 是的。從明年起，我要去英國讀中學。

> **TIP**
> In the phrase "從……起"，起 means "the start". It indicates the starting time of an event or an occurrence, which is stated in the following phrase.

A: 你們什麼時候開始放假？

B: 從下星期三起，我們就開始放假了。

 **PRACTICE IT**

Using sentence structure 1, complete the dialogues with the helping phrases.

1. A: 我想做運動，不過一個人沒有意思。

   B: _____

2. A: 現在你媽媽還是每天送你去上學嗎？

   B: 不，_____

3. A: 老師，我們什麼時候開始學寫中文字？

   B: _____

Group A	Group B
第三課	自己去上學了
十歲	開始寫中文字
明天	可以一起去慢跑

2	她聽不懂英文	我會幫她的忙。
	的時候，	
	上課有問題	我們可以問老師。

dǒng (above 懂)

A: 我有一點累，可是功課還沒做完。

B: 有一點累**的時候**，就到外面走一走，休息一下。

A: 有的時候我也會不開心。

B: 不開心**的時候**，你可以給我打電話。

> **TIP** The phrase "⋯⋯的時候" indicates a situation. The following clause indicates a possible solution to the situation.

PRACTICE IT

Using sentence structure 2, complete the dialogues with the helping phrases.

1. A: 我從上個月起，開始學日文了。 rì wén

   B: <u>想練習日文的時候打電話給我。</u>

2. A: 我和小明每個星期都會一起去打球。

   B: 我也喜歡打球，<u>下次要打球的時候找我一起練習。</u>

3. A: 今天我坐公車去學校。車上人好多。

   B: <u>要坐公車的時候早一點出門。</u>

Group A

要坐公車

下次要打球

想練習日文 rì wén

Group B

早一點出門

找我一起練習

打電話給我

Go 500 **WANT TO LEARN MORE?**

Check out the Text > Sentence Pattern section on the Go500 CD.

 **Listening**

Go 500

Text > Dialogue section

 A Listen to the Go500 CD for the dialogue and answer the following multiple-choice questions.

1. 以晴現在＿＿＿＿＿＿＿。 B

(A) 七歲　(B) 在讀中學 (zhōng xué)　(C) 學了七年中文

2. 以晴在哪裡出生 (chū shēng)？ A

(A) 美國 (měi guó)　(B) 臺灣 (tái wān)　(C) 中國 (zhōng guó)

3. 以晴的爸爸媽媽從哪裡來？  B

(A) 以晴的媽媽是美國人，爸爸從臺灣 (tái wān)來。

(B) 以晴的爸爸是美國人，媽媽從臺灣 (tái wān)來。

(C) 以晴的爸爸媽媽都在美國 (měi guó)出生 (chū shēng)。

4. 為什麼同學叫以晴跟她的朋友「High Five」？ C

(A) 他們常常一起上課。

(B) 他們常常用手做「High Five」。

(C) 他們有五個人，一開心就說「High Five」。

5. 為什麼以晴覺得學中文很有用？  C

(A) 有很多人學中文。

(B) 老師用中文上課。

(C) 可以幫別的同學的忙。

New Words

出生 (chū shēng) | to be born

中學 (zhōng xué) | secondary school

初中 (chū zhōng) | junior high school

B Number the following texts in the correct order to form a coherent conversation.

4 老師：為什麼同學叫你們五個人「High Five」?

以晴：因為我們五個人常常一起參加活動，

_____。

---

1 老師：以晴，妳現在幾nián jí年級?

以晴：我現在七年級，_____，我是zhōng xué shēng中學生了。

---

3 老師：妳覺得學中文有用嗎?

以晴：我覺得學中文很有用。我們學校有很多

ESL 的學生，_____，有的從

tái wān臺灣來，他們的英文都_____不好_____。

他們_____的時候，我可以

幫他們的忙。

---

2 老師：妳爸媽_____?

以晴：我爸爸是美國人，我

媽媽從tái wān臺灣來，我

_____chū shēng出生。

C Listen to the conversation on the Go500 CD again, and fill in the blanks.

 **Playing**

Form groups of four and role-play the scenario. You may use the sentence structures provided below.

CHARACTERS:

媽媽, 張靜, 久美子, 以晴

SCENARIO:

久美子 and 張靜 are at Sunny's (以晴) house for a play date. 久美子 would like to invite 張靜 and 以晴 to spend the night at her house on Saturday. However, Sunny's mother has some reservations about it, and so the three girls are trying to persuade her to agree to it.

SENTENCE STRUCTURES:

1. 從……起……

2. ……的時候，……

3. 有人……，也有人……

4. 你覺得……最好？

Learn about the
Chinese Language & Culture

你正在看的這本書，文字是從左邊寫到右邊，從上面寫到下面。如果你想要讀（dú）一讀（dú），你就要找到每一頁（yè）最上面的字，再從左邊的第一個字開始。

不過（bú guò）不是每一本中文書都是這樣的。以前（yǐ qián）中國（zhōng guó）人把字刻（kè）在竹片（zhú piàn）上，因為竹片（zhú piàn）瘦瘦長長的，所以得從上面刻（kè）到下面，刻（kè）完第一片（piàn），就先放在右邊，再刻（kè）第二片（piàn）。第二片（piàn）刻（kè）完再刻（kè）第三片（piàn），等每一個字都刻（kè）完了，就用繩子（shéng zi）把竹片（zhú piàn）串（chuàn）起來。

你看，「冊（cè）」這個字像不像是用繩子（shéng zi）把每一片竹片串（piàn zhú piàn chuàn）起來的樣子？這些串（chuàn）起來的竹（zhú）片（piàn），會從最左邊向右卷（juǎn）起來。所以看從上寫到下的中文書時，要從最右邊的句子開始看。

寫書法（shū fǎ）的時候，也是從右邊寫到左邊，從上面寫到下面。

---

*頁 page   刻 carve   竹片 bamboo slates   片 piece   繩子 string; rope   串 string together   冊 book; volume
捲 roll up   以前 in the past; before   書法 calligraphy

Work It Out

We may share similar interests or character traits with our friends. Even if we don't, our friends will always think of us and help us out. The friends we make in school are often our study mates, and we may participate in various activities together. Besides our family, friends provide a warm and loving environment for us to grow and learn. They also make our lives more enriching and meaningful.

TASK

My Friends and I

1 Complete the table with information about yourself.

2 Interview your friends. Identify three friends who share your interests and hobbies, and take the same courses as you this semester.

名字	興趣	不喜歡做的事	今年選了哪些課？
我			
1.			
2.			
3.			

LEARNING LOG

I can...

		Excellent	Good	Fair	Need Improvement
1	introduce my friends by stating the countries they come from and talk about our shared activities.	○	○	○	○
2	use the structure "從……起，……" to pinpoint the starting point of an event or situation.	○	○	○	○
3	use the structure "……的時候，……" to offer a solution to a problem.	○	○	○	○
4	explain why some Chinese text is written from top to bottom, and from right to left.	○	○	○	○
5	write 年級, 不過, 原來, and 讀書.	○	○	○	○

我的朋友
My Friends

My Goals

1 Introduce my friends in Chinese
2 Indicate that an event only occurs during a stated time
3 Describe an action done to another and the underlying intention
4 Describe a situation where there is no exception
5 See how friendship can develop despite differences in age and gender
6 Become familiar with vocabulary associated with one's personality

1 What are these people doing?
2 Are your friends about your age?

A Complete the following sentences according to the corresponding pictures.

我有很多好朋友，有＿＿＿＿＿＿＿＿＿＿＿＿＿，

也有＿＿＿＿＿＿＿＿＿＿。

白爺爺是我的朋友。我一有時間，就＿＿＿＿＿＿＿

＿＿＿＿＿＿＿＿＿＿＿。

圓圓也是我的朋友。圓圓很可愛，她只要＿＿＿＿

＿＿＿＿＿＿＿，就會一邊＿＿＿＿＿＿＿＿＿＿，

一邊＿＿＿＿＿＿＿＿＿。

我有＿＿＿＿＿＿＿＿＿＿＿＿。

有了這些朋友，我每天都開心。

B Read your completed sentences aloud to your classmates.

xìng bié
性别
(gender)

nán hái
男孩
(boy)

nǚ hái
女孩
(girl)

nán xìng
男性
(male)

nǚ xìng
女性
(female)

New Words

nǚ hái 女孩	girl
nán xìng 男性 wài xiàng 外向	extroverted
nèi xiàng 内向	introverted

Which terms would you use
to describe your classmates?

wài xiàng
外向

hào kè
好客
(hospitable)

kāi lǎng
開朗
开
(cheerful)

wēn róu
温温柔
(gentle)

gè xìng
个個性
(personality)

nèi xiàng
内向

lè guān
乐樂觀观
(optimistic)

dú lì
独獨立
(independent)

chéng shí
诚誠實实
(honest)

hài xiū
害羞
(shy)

yōu mò
幽默
(humorous)

wēn hé
温和
(mild)

tǐ tiē
体體贴
(considerate)

zì xìn
自信
(confident)

fù zé
负負责责
(responsible)

bèi dòng
被動动
(passive)

zhǔ dòng
主動动
(take initiative)

dà fāng
大方
(generous)

huó pō
活潑泼
(vivacious)

SCENARIO: Mother often says that 以晴 is an extroverted girl who enjoys making friends. Let us read about how 以晴 feels about this.

媽媽說得很對，我是一個外向的女孩，喜歡找人說話，很容易交朋友。我的朋友有老的，有小的，有男的，有女的，每一國人都有。

我的「老」朋友是白爺爺。他是英國人，他姓White，今年八十三歲。白爺爺很喜歡學新東西，他常常問我一些電腦的問題。他也喜歡中華文化，常常去中國餐館吃中國菜，也常常問媽媽很多中華文化的問題。他會用中文叫我「以晴」，還要我用中文叫他「白爺爺」。

我的「小」朋友是圓圓，她今年三歲，長得圓圓胖胖的，很可愛。圓圓的爸爸和媽媽是越南人，他們開洗衣店，❶從早忙到晚，只有星期日休息。有的時候，❷他們會把圓圓送來我家，讓

我照顧她。圓圓很喜歡唱歌和跳舞，最愛看卡通，常常一邊看，一邊唱。

我還有其他三個好朋友，牠們不是「人」。「雪球」是一隻狗，「紅紅」和「藍藍」是兩條魚。照顧小魚很容易，只要餵牠們，給牠們一個乾淨的家就可以了。可是，照顧「雪球」不容易。我每天都要帶牠去散步，還要和牠說話、跟牠玩。不過，養了「雪球」以後，因為每天都要和牠一起運動，我的身體更健康了。

每天，我都會和我的好朋友們說話。我每天都很開心，天天「天晴」。

New Words

shuō huà 說話 — talk	jiāo péng yǒu 交朋友 — make friends	yì xiē 一些 — some	zhōng huá 中華 — Chinese
wén huà 文化 — culture	cān guǎn 餐館 — restaurant	yuè nán rén 越南人 — Vietnamese	xǐ yī diàn 洗衣店 — Laundromat
qí tā 其他 — other	gēn 跟 — with	yǐ hòu 以後 — after; later	

Exercises

True or False?

Answer the questions according to the passage.

對　錯

1. 以晴是一個外向（wài xiàng）的女孩（nǚ hái），她有很多朋友。　〇　〇
2. 白爺爺的中文不好，所以他常常問以晴中文問題。　〇　〇
3. 圓圓只有星期日才能到以晴家玩。　〇　〇
4. 照顧「紅紅」和「藍藍」比照顧「雪球」難。　〇　〇
5. 因為以晴常常跟（gēn）雪球說話（shuō huà），所以她的身體更健康了。　〇　〇

Think & Discuss

Work in pairs and answer the questions in Chinese.

1. 為什麼以晴說她每天都很開心，天天「天晴」？
2. 以晴在這一課介紹了哪些朋友？她的朋友們叫什麼名字？
3. 你有哪些好朋友？介紹他們給大家認識。

Culture Link

We typically make friends with people around our own age as we are likely to share similar interests and social circles. However, 以晴 is friends with 白爺爺 and 圓圓, whose ages are vastly different from hers. 忘年之交 (wàng nián zhī jiāo) is an idiom used to describe friendships which are unaffected by vast age differences. Literally, it means that when a strong friendship is forged between two people, the differences associated with their age disparity are easily forgotten. About 1800 years ago, Ni Heng (禰衡 Ní Héng) was barely twenty years old and Kong Rong (孔融 Kǒng Róng) was over fifty years old. Yet, Kong Rong was impressed with Ni Heng's character and capability and the two forged a strong friendship despite their age gap. A friendship like this may be beneficial in that the younger party may learn from the experiences of the older one. The older party may also feel younger due to the energy and youthful vibe emanated by the younger one.

TALK ABOUT IT

Do you have a friend who is much older or younger than you? Who is the person? How did the two of you meet? What activities do you engage in together?

Language Focus

1

從	早	忙	到	晚，	只有	星期日	（才）	休息。
	去年	上課		現在，		放寒暑假前		考試。

A: 你怎麼現在才吃飯？

B: 我**從**十一點忙**到**現在，**只有**沒客人的時候能吃飯。

A: 他的學校很遠。他住學校嗎？

B: **從**星期一**到**星期五他都住在學校，**只有**週末**才**回家。

TIP

This sentence structure consists of two parts. The first part "從……到……" indicates a specific time span. If used independently, the second part "只有……" stipulates a restriction by a condition. However, in this sentence structure, it indicates an exception to the norm. This sentence structure conveys that within the stated time frame, only on the condition stipulated by the phrase 只有 will the situation or action occur. It also implies that the situation or action occurs very infrequently and is the exception rather than the norm. The word 才 can be omitted.

PRACTICE IT

Using sentence structure 1, complete the dialogues with the helping pharses.

1. A: 你媽媽說你星期天要上班，你天天都要工作嗎？

   B: 不！ *我不是天天工作。*

2. A: 你弟弟真認真，他不休息嗎？

   B: *他也有休息的時候。*

Group A	Group B
從星期一休息到星期五	吃飯的時候才休息
從早學到晚	週末上班

	他們	把	圓圓送來我家，	讓	我	照顧她。
2	以晴		雪球帶到公園，		牠	運動運動。

他們**把**孩子送去臺灣，
讓他們認識中華文化。
zhōng huá wén huà

老師**把**作業還給學生，
讓他們看看哪裡寫錯了。

TIP The clause introduced by 把 states an action done to a recipient known to the listener. The word 讓 can mean a result or request, or that permission has been granted. In the first example, the subject (他們) has imposed an action (送圓圓來我家) on a recipient (我), and the motive behind the action is conveyed at the end of the sentence (要我照顧圓圓).

PRACTICE IT

Based on the scenarios, make sentences using sentence structure 2 and the helping phrases.

1. 他帶介紹越南的書去學校……
   他帶介紹越南的書去学校，给他的朋友看。

2. 我給我的朋友介紹以思……
   我给我的朋友介绍以思，让大家问他很多的問題。

3. 爸爸做好早餐了……
   爸爸做好早餐了，让大家快一点来吃。

媽媽可以多睡一點
同學們看
他們認識認識

WANT TO LEARN MORE?
Check out the Text > Sentence Pattern section on the Go500 CD.

Listening

Go 500

Text > Dialogue section

SCENARIO: 張靜 has been calling 以晴 on the telephone after school for a few days, but 以晴 has not been home. Today, 張靜 finally manages to contact 以晴.

A Listen to the Go500 CD for the dialogue and answer the following multiple-choice questions. Question 2 and 3 may have more than one answer.

1. 以晴星期六要教誰電腦？ `B`

   (A) 外公　**(B)** 白爺爺　**(C)** 張靜的爺爺

2. 我們可以怎麼介紹白爺爺？ `A`

   (A) 住在以晴家附近　　　**(B)** 住在英國

   (C) 喜歡中華文化 (zhōng huá wén huà)　　　**(D)** 是以晴的外公

   (E) 大以晴十三歲

3. 我們可以怎麼介紹圓圓？ `B`

   (A) 是以晴的妹妹　　　**(B)** 長得圓圓胖胖的

   (C) 小以晴三歲　　　　**(D)** 會照顧以晴

   (E) 有的時候會去以晴家

4. 張靜找到以晴的時候是星期幾？ `A`

   (A) 星期三　**(B)** 星期四　**(C)** 星期五

5. 為什麼張靜常常找不到以晴？ `C`

   (A) 以晴不喜歡打電話。

   (B) 以晴參加很多活動，不在家。

   (C) 以晴都在跟她的「老」朋友、(gēn) 「小」朋友和「動物」朋友 說話 (shuō huà)。

New Words

老先生 (lǎo xiān shēng)	old man
越南 (yuè nán)	Vietnam

B Number the following texts in the correct order to form a coherent conversation.

〔　〕 張靜：星期三我打電話給妳，妳不在，星期四打電
　　　　　話給妳，妳也不在，妳真忙！

　　　以晴：對不起！我 _因為出去找朋友說_，所以常常
　　　　　　不在家。媽媽說我很 _忙_ ，❸天天都要找
　　　　　shuō huà
　　　　　朋友說話，她 _說我个性外向_ ！

〔　〕 張靜：妳說妳星期六要去教「白爺爺」電腦，「白
　　　　　　爺爺」是誰？是妳的外公嗎？

　　　以晴：白爺爺不是我的外公，他是 Mr. White，他 _是_
　　　　　　我的老朋友 。白爺爺是一個八十三歲的
　　　　　lǎo xiān shēng
　　　　　英國老先生。他喜歡 _說中文_ ，也要我
　　　　　用中文 叫他「白爺爺」。他是我的「老」朋友。

〔　〕 張靜：天天都要找朋友說話？天天都找得到朋友嗎？
　　　　　　　　　　　shuō huà
　　　以晴：我有「老」朋友、「小」朋友、「爸爸」朋
　　　　　　友、「媽媽」朋友，還有「 _白_ 」朋友。

〔　〕 張靜：圓圓又是誰？
　　　　　　　　　　yuè nán　　nǔ hái
　　　以晴：圓圓是一個越南小女孩，只有三歲。她長得
　　　　　　圓圓胖胖 的，很可愛。她是我 _朋友_
　　　　　　的女儿 。因為我沒有妹妹，我常常要媽
　　　　　　媽 _把她接来我家_ ，我
　　　　　　會照顧圓圓，和她一起玩。

C Listen to the conversation on the Go500 CD again, and fill in the blanks.

38　我的朋友

Language Focus

3

（我）	天天	都	要找朋友說話。 shuō huà
我的朋友	個個		外向。 wài xiàng

A: 張大山寫的書怎麼樣？

B: 我覺得他寫的書本本都好看。

A: 這家店的衣服怎麼樣？

B: 這家店的衣服件件都便宜。

TIP The reduplication of a monosyllabic measure word conveys the meaning of "every". The structure that typically follows the repeated measure word is "都 + Verb / Adjective / Clause". However, 都 may be omitted at times, as reflected in the last line of the reading passage in this chapter—天天「天晴」.

 **PRACTICE IT**

Using sentence structure 3, complete the dialogues with the helping phrases.

1. A: 牠們是爸爸送我的小貓。

   B: 這些小貓 _____

2. A: 這個學校的學生多嗎？

   B: 很多！你看那些教室 _____

3. A: 張老師，今年的學生怎麼樣？

   B: 今年的學生 _____

Go 500 **WANT TO LEARN MORE?**

Check out the Text > Sentence Pattern section on the Go500 CD.

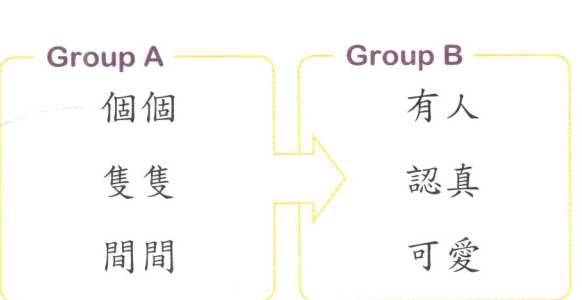

Group A	Group B
個個	有人
隻隻	認真
間間	可愛

Form groups of four and role-play the scenario. You may use the sentence structures provided below.

CHARACTERS:

張靜, 久美子, 安地, 以晴

SCENARIO:

As Ming's (阿明) birthday is approaching, 張靜, 久美子, 安地, and 以晴 would like to buy him a present. They are discussing when and where they can go to get the present but 以晴 simply cannot find time in her busy schedule to join them.

SENTENCE STRUCTURES:

1. 從……到……，只有……（才）……

2. 把……讓……

3. （Reduplication of measure word） 都……

4. 一……，就……

5. 只要……，就……

Learn about the Chinese Language & Culture

你看過這些東西嗎？

你知道這些東西有個同樣的名字，叫做「印章（yìn zhāng）」嗎？

在有些國家（guó jiā），印章（yìn zhāng）是很重要的，有的時候蓋印章（gài yìn zhāng）就跟簽名（gēn qiān míng）一樣，有的時候蓋印章（gài yìn zhāng）比簽名（qiān míng）更有用。

蓋印章（gài yìn zhāng）可以讓大家知道這個東西是誰的，或是蓋印章（gài yìn zhāng）的人同意（tóng yì）一件事。

中國有一位皇帝（huáng dì）很喜歡蓋印章（gài yìn zhāng），只要是他拿到的東西，他都會在上面蓋（gài）上他的印章（yìn zhāng）。如果你以後（yǐ hòu）看到中國的畫，可以找一找有沒有這位皇帝（huáng dì）的印章（yìn zhāng）。

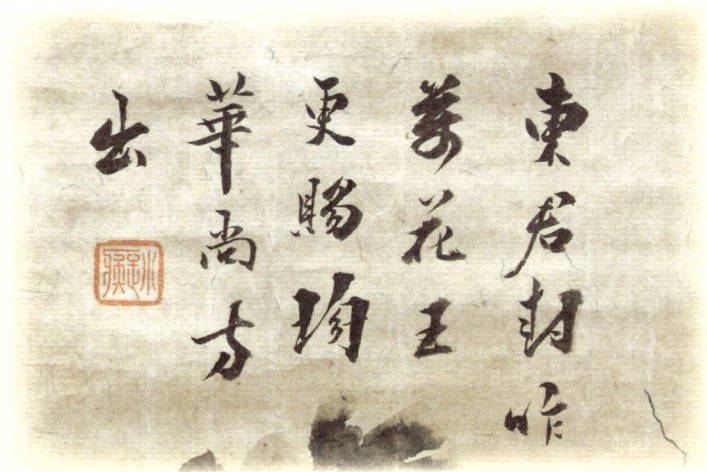

*印章 seal　國家 country　蓋 affix　簽名 signature　同意 approve　皇帝 emperor

Work It Out

以晴 has many friends—her schoolmates, her old friend, 白爺爺, her young friend, 圓圓, her parents, and even her pet, 雪球. With such a diverse social circle, she enjoys a variety of activities which makes her life enjoyable and enriching. Do you have such a diverse social circle too?

TASK Guess Who ?

1 Write your name on a small slip of paper, fold it up, and give it to the teacher.

2 The teacher randomly distributes a slip to each student.

3 Get into pairs and withhold the name on your paper.

4 Describe the person on your slip of paper (in terms of his personality, hobbies, interests, capabilities, classes, etc) for the other to guess who he or she is.

5 The teacher may ask two or three students to describe their friends (without revealing the name) in front of the class for everybody to guess who they are.

LEARNING LOG

I can...

	Excellent	Good	Fair	Need Improvement
1 introduce my friends.	○	○	○	○
2 describe my friends' personalities.	○	○	○	○
3 use the structures "從……到……，只有……" and "(subject) 把……讓……" to form sentences.	○	○	○	○
4 use "(reduplication of measure word) 都……" to convey that there is no exception in the stated context.	○	○	○	○
5 write 內向, 越南人, 中華 and 以後.	○	○	○	○

我愛看的書
My Favorite Books

1 Do you like reading?
2 What books do you enjoy reading?

My Goals

1 Recommend a book in Chinese
2 Express the increasing intensity of a matter
3 Convey that somebody is requesting or demanding that somebody else performs a task
4 Recognize various forms of Chinese poetry
5 Become familiar with vocabulary used to talk about books

A Based on the pictures, complete the following sentences using the helping phrases given.

大明是一個愛看書的孩子，只要

＿＿＿＿＿＿＿＿＿＿＿＿＿＿＿＿＿，

他就＿＿＿＿＿＿＿＿＿＿＿＿＿＿＿。

他從＿＿＿＿＿＿到＿＿＿＿＿＿，

只有＿＿＿＿＿＿＿＿＿＿＿＿＿＿。

你問他最喜歡看什麼書，他說：

「我覺得什麼＿＿＿＿＿都＿＿＿＿＿

＿＿＿。我＿＿＿＿＿＿都＿＿＿＿＿

＿＿＿＿＿＿。」

B Read your completed sentences aloud to your classmates.

Vocabulary Builder

shī	xiǎo shuō	shén huà	tóng huà	yù yán
詩 诗	小說 说	神話 话 (myth)	童話 (children's stories; fairy tales)	寓言 (fable)

gù shì shū	kē pǔ shū	tú huà shū	màn huà shū	zá zhì
故事書 书	科普書 书	圖 图 畫書 画 书	漫畫書	雜誌 杂 志 (magazine)
(popular science book)		(picture book)	(comic book)	

tuī lǐ	kǒng bù	qí huàn
推理 (logic and reason)	恐怖 (horror)	奇幻 (fantasy)

ài qíng	wǔ xiá	lì shǐ
愛情 爱 (romance)	武俠 俠 (sword-fighting)	歷史 历 (history)

shū míng	zuò zhě	huì zhě
書名 书 (title)	作者 (author)	繪者 绘 (illustrator)

yì zhě fān yì	chū bǎn shè
譯者/翻譯 译 译 (translator)	出版社 (publisher)

Genre Chain

1 Students take turn to name three books they like and the teacher lists them on the board.

2 Talk about the genres of these books.

3 Form a circle. The teacher begins by naming a book that has just been recommended. A student has to state the genre of the book, and then name another book for the next student. This goes on until everybody has had a turn.

4 Students who get the genre wrong are eliminated until the winner is left.

New Words

shī 詩	poetry
xiǎo shuō 小說	novel
gù shì shū 故事書	story book

Example:

Teacher:	Frog Prince
Student 1:	童話. Harry Potter.
Student 2:	小說. Sherlock Holmes.
Student 3:	推理小說...

SCENARIO: Sunny's mother has always encouraged her to read and she has cultivated a love for books.

從我小時候起，媽媽就常常買有趣的中文故事
書給我看，也會念給我聽；她希望我可以一邊看，
一邊聽，一邊學中文字。媽媽說，因為中文比英文
難學，所以她要先教我中文。

除了故事書，我也喜歡看短短的中文詩和英文
詩，因為詩的字不多，容易看，容易懂。我喜歡聽
媽媽念詩，有時候她會一邊念一邊跳舞，有時候我
會跟她一起跳。

上小學以後，我最喜歡看《十萬個為什麼》。這些書教我很多東西，讓我可以回答很多問題。五年級的時候，老師要我們看小說，那時候我不喜歡看，❶因為字太多了，而且有些小說裡面有壞人，故事很可怕，讓人很緊張。不過，❷現在我越來越喜歡看小說了。有些小說寫得好像真的，好像在寫我和我的朋友。好看的小說真的太棒了。

現在我愛看的英文書很多，Anne of Green Gables 是我最喜歡的一本書。我愛看的中文書很少，因為我認識的中文字不夠多。那些我想看的書，裡面的字太多又太難，所以❸媽媽要我把中文學好。她說，很多有趣的中文書比 Harry Potter 還好看。為了要看那些有趣的書，我每星期上中文學校，我每天用心學中文。

New Words

小時候 xiǎo shí hòu	when one was younger	念 niàn	read out	十萬 shí wàn	one hundred thousand
這些 zhè xiē	these	而且 ér qiě	furthermore	壞人 huài rén	villain
故事 gù shì	story	可怕 kě pà	frightening	越 yuè	more
好像 hǎo xiàng	seem	棒 bàng	excellent	裡面 lǐ miàn	inside

Exercises

Answer the questions according to the passage.

對　錯

1. 為了要看中文書，以晴每天用心學中文。　✓　○

2. 以晴喜歡念詩，因為詩的字少，容易懂。
<small>niàn shī</small>　<small>shī</small>　✓　✓~~

3. 以晴念詩的時候，媽媽會一起跳舞。
<small>niàn shī</small>　✓　○

4. 以晴小時候不喜歡看小說，因為有的小說
寫得很像真的。
<small>xiǎo shí hòu</small>　<small>xiǎo shuō</small>　<small>xiǎo shuō</small>　○　✓

5. 以晴現在喜歡的英文書比中文書多。　✓　○

Think & Discuss

Work in pairs and answer the questions in Chinese.

1. 以晴為什麼從小就看中文書？

2. 為什麼以晴以前不喜歡看小說，可是現在越來越喜歡？
<small>xiǎo shuō</small>　<small>yuè</small>　<small>yuè</small>

3. 你看過哪些中文書？你覺得自己學中文用心嗎？
為什麼？

Culture  Link

Do you know these stories? Tell the stories to your friends.

Language Focus

TIP
Used between two clauses, the clause that follows 而且 conveys a greater intensity than the first. When one uses such a sentence construction, it is intended that the second clause be emphasized, as the message conveyed in this clause is more important than the first.

1

小說（xiǎo shuō）字太多了，

那本書很有意思，

而且（ér qiě）　有些小說故事（xiǎo shuō gù shì）很可怕（kě pà），讓人很緊張。

能學很多中文字。

A: 那個女孩好像（hǎo xiàng）不喜歡跟我們說話。

B: 她才來新學校，**而且**（ér qiě）她很內向，所以不常和大家說話。

A: 為什麼你喜歡看中文小說（xiǎo shuō）？

B: 因為小說（xiǎo shuō）很有意思，**而且**（ér qiě）我還能邊看邊學中文。

PRACTICE IT

Using sentence structure 1, complete the dialogues with the helping phrases.

1. A: 你的中文真不錯。

   B: _____

   _____

2. A: 我們不出去玩嗎？

   B: _____

   _____

3. A: 以晴的朋友真多！

   B: _____

   _____

Group A

小時候（xiǎo shí hòu）住在臺灣

(个)個性外向

有功課（課）要做

Group B

天氣（气）不太好

每天上中文課

喜歡（欢）幫（帮）朋友的忙

2	我	越來越 (yuè yuè)	喜歡	看小說 (xiǎo shuō) 了。
	她		會	照顧小狗。

媽媽不在家三天了，妹妹越來越 (yuè yuè) 想媽媽了。

弟弟越來越 (yuè yuè) 不喜歡上數學課了。

TIP "越來越(不)" indicates that the subject's feelings, capability, viewpoint, etc towards something is increasing or decreasing in intensity with time. In example 1, the speaker enjoys reading novels more and more as time passes.

PRACTICE IT

Using sentence structure 2, rewrite the sentences with the helping phrases.

1. 以晴的詩 (shī) 寫得比去年好。

   以晴越來越懂得寫詩 (shī) 了。 _____ （懂得）

2. 以前大關不知道怎麼照顧妹妹，現在不一樣了。

   _____ （會）

3. 以前舅舅一年去旅行一次，現在一年去兩次。

   _____ （常）

媽媽	要	我	把	中文學好。
老師		學生		作業寫完。

3

爸爸叫哥哥好好地讀書。

➔ 爸爸要哥哥把書讀好。

老師請學生清理教室。

➔ 老師要學生把教室清理乾淨。

TIP

This sentence structure consists of two parts. In the first part, 要 means a request or an order for somebody to do something. In the second part, 把 introduces the action that is requested or demanded. This sentence structure conveys a situation where the subject is requesting or demanding that the object completes a task.

PRACTICE IT

Using sentence structure 3, rewrite the sentences with the helping phrases.

1. 爸爸叫弟弟拿衣服。

爸爸叫弟弟把衣服拿來。　　　　（拿來）

2. 姊姊說吃完飯以後要洗碗筷。

姐姐說要吃完飯以後把洗乾淨。　　（洗乾淨）

3. 奶奶叫妹妹吃完碗裡的飯。

奶奶要妹妹把碗裡的飯吃完　　　（吃完）

WANT TO LEARN MORE?

Check out the Text > Sentence Pattern section on the Go500 CD.

Listening

Go 500

Text > Dialogue section

SCENARIO: In class, 以晴 learns about English poetry, which she is very interested in. After class, her teacher speaks to her.

A Listen to the Go500 CD for the dialogue and answer the following multiple-choice questions.

1. 以晴為什麼喜歡詩（shī）？　　　　　　　　*C*

(A) 詩（shī）的句子很長。

(B) 詩（shī）很容易懂。

(C) 媽媽會念詩（niàn shī）給以晴聽。

2. 以晴現在不喜歡看什麼？　　　　　　　　*B*

(A) 詩（shī）　(B) 小說（xiǎo shuō）　(C) 中文書

3. 以晴現在為什麼不喜歡看中文書？　　　　*A*

(A) 她看不懂。

(B) 書裡的故事（gù shì）太可怕（kě pà）。

(C) 書裡的故事（gù shì）沒有意思。

4. 以晴現在為什麼喜歡看小說（xiǎo shuō）？　*B*

(A) 媽媽現在會念小說（niàn xiǎo shuō）給以晴聽。

(B) 小說（xiǎo shuō）就像在寫自己和朋友的故事（gù shì）。

(C) 朋友把好看的小說（xiǎo shuō）介紹給以晴看。

5. 以晴想介紹什麼書給朋友？　　　　　　　*C*

(A) 詩（shī）　(B) 好書　(C) 小說（xiǎo shuō）

New Words

卻（què） | but

B Number the following texts in the correct order to form a coherent conversation.

2 老師：小時候妳讀了很多中文書，為什麼長大了，妳卻不喜歡看中文書了？

以晴：小時候，媽媽幫我的忙，念書給我聽。現在我覺得中文書太難，而且，我每星期才上兩個小時的中文課，＿＿＿＿＿＿＿＿＿＿。我想看的書太難，如果你＿＿＿＿＿＿，就不會想看。

老師：妳覺得什麼書是好書？

以晴：我覺得好書要＿＿＿＿＿，會讓人喜歡看，也讓我＿＿＿＿＿＿＿＿＿＿。

老師：以晴，妳為什麼喜歡詩？

以晴：詩的字不多，＿＿＿＿＿＿，＿＿＿＿＿＿，也容易寫，❹我可以寫得長，也可以寫得短。

老師：現在妳為什麼喜歡看小說？

以晴：有些小說裡有＿＿＿＿＿＿＿＿＿，很好看，也很趣。有些小說好像在寫＿＿＿＿＿＿＿＿＿，所以現在我喜歡看小說。

C Listen to the conversation on the Go500 CD again, and fill in the blanks.

In poetry, a poet uses regular sentence structures, concise language, rhythm, and rhyme to express his imagination as well as his views and observations of the world. In doing so, he creates a piece of literary work.

About 1400 years ago, Chinese poets were fond of writing poems which consisted of only four lines. Each line was made up of either five or seven characters. Though these poems are short, they are meaningful and remain popular today.

TALK ABOUT IT Do you know these two poems? Do you like them? Why?

---

xiǎo
春 曉
Dawn in Spring

mèng hào rán
孟 浩 然

mián   xiǎo
春 眠 不 覺 曉 ,
(Asleep in Spring, I missed the break of dawn)

chù chù   tí
處 處 聞 啼 鳥 。
(Until I heard birds singing everywhere)

yè   shēng
夜 來 風 雨 聲 ,
(The night had endured the wind and rain)

花 落 知 多 少 。
(One wonders how many flowers had fallen in the storm)

---

yè
靜 夜 思
Thoughts on a Quiet Night

lǐ bái
李 白

床 前 明 月 光 ,
(Before my bed, the moon shines brightly)

yí sì   shuāng
疑 似 地 上 霜 。
(I think that it is frost on the ground)

jǔ tóu
舉 頭 望 明 月 ,
(I raise my head to gaze at the bright moon)

dī tóu   gù xiāng
低 頭 思 故 鄉 。
(I lower my head, thinking of home)

There is another kind of Chinese verse known as 打油詩 (dǎ yóu shī) which is very interesting and easy to understand and recite. Can you guess what the verse on the right is describing?

jì xiǎo lán
紀 曉 嵐

piàn   piàn   piàn
一 片 兩 片 三 四 片 ,
(One, two, three, four flakes)

piàn   piàn   piàn
五 片 六 片 七 八 片 ,
(Five, six, seven, eight flakes)

piàn   piàn   piàn
九 片 十 片 十 一 片 ,
(nine, ten, eleven flakes)

fēi rù cǎo cóng jiē bú jiàn
飛 入 草 叢 皆 不 見 。
(Fluttering into the undergrowth, they disappear)

Language Focus

我	可以	寫得長，	也可以	寫得短。
我		上午做，		下午做。

4

A: 老師，哪裡可以找到這本書？

B: 你可以去圖書館看，也可以去書店買。

A: 我什麼時候可以去找你？

B: 都可以，你可以早上來，也可以下午來。你想晚上來也沒關係。

> **TIP** In this sentence structure 可以 means "can" or "may". The phrases after 可以 convey the possibilities to a particular situation, indicating that the speaker is rather flexible with his options.

 **PRACTICE IT**

Using sentence structure 4, complete the dialogues with the helping phrases.

1. A: 下午你要自己去叔叔家嗎？

   B: _____

2. A: 現在要讓表姊知道比賽的成績嗎？

   B: _____

3. A: 你看書看得很慢嗎？

   B: _____

Group A	Group B
下午去	晚一點再跟她說
現在跟她說	看得快
看得慢	明天跟你一起去

Role Playing

Form groups of three and role-play the scenario. You may use the sentence structures provided below.

CHARACTERS:

以晴, 久美子, 安地

SCENARIO:

During recess, 久美子 and 安地 find 以晴 reading a book in the classroom. When 以晴 recommends the book to them, 久美子 and 安地 become rather interested in reading it. They discuss who gets to borrow the book first when 以晴 finishes reading it.

SENTENCE STRUCTURES:

1. 越來越⋯⋯
2. 可以⋯⋯，也可以⋯⋯
3. ⋯⋯而且⋯⋯
4. 要⋯⋯把⋯⋯
5. 從⋯⋯到⋯⋯，只有⋯⋯

Learn about the Chinese Language & Culture

這個星期天早上以晴想跟久美子去*慢跑，以安也想跟朋友去打球，但是有人得先把*院子打掃乾淨，才能出去。以安起來後，發現以晴出去了，又看到一張給他的*字條。

看完字條以後，以安氣得說：「怎麼可以這樣呢！」卻還是去打掃院子了。你知道為什麼嗎？請念出字條每一句的第一個字，你就會知道以安為什麼會去打掃院子了。

作者把他想說的話，放在每個句子的第一個字，每個句子有自己的意思，讓讀詩的人不容易讀出作者的意思，這就是「*藏頭詩」。

寫藏頭詩的人不但要會寫，讀的人也要*聰明才行。想不想也來寫藏頭詩？

> 今天起得早，
> 天氣真是好，
> 你妹去慢跑。
> 打球行不行？
> 掃完地再走。

---

*慢跑 jogging　　院子 courtyard　　字條 message on a slip of paper　　藏 conceal　　聰明 smart

Work It Out

Do you enjoy reading books? What kinds of stories do you enjoy—suspenseful ones, easy-reading ones, or funny ones? While reading is meaningful, telling a story is even more meaningful and interesting.

TASK
Composing A Creative Story

1 Try crafting an outrageous and exaggerated story with your friends using the introduction provided below.

2 As a class, take turns to contribute a sentence each to continue the story to make it as outrageous as possible. The teacher may suggest some sentence structures to be used, but they are not mandatory.

3 At the end of the lesson, record the story in your composition book.

很久很久以前，有一個男孩叫阿明。
阿明非常喜歡看書，他從早看到晚……

_____

_____

LEARNING LOG

I can...

	Excellent	Good	Fair	Need Improvement
1 recommend my favorite books to others.	○	○	○	○
2 use the sentence structures "……而且……", "越來越……", and "可以……，也可以……" to form sentences.	○	○	○	○
3 use "要……把……" to express the idea that somebody is asking somebody else to complete a task.	○	○	○	○
4 read the poems introduced in this lesson and explain what they mean.	○	○	○	○
5 write 這些, 故事, 可怕, and 而且.	○	○	○	○

我們去買菜
Let's Go to the Market

1 Have you been to a traditional market?
2 How is it different from a supermarket?

My Goals

1 Talk about my experience at the market
2 Convey a consequence that one is afraid of or unwilling to suffer
3 Use adjectives to state the criteria for an item
4 Explain the origins of pictographic characters and ideograms
5 Become familiar with vocabulary associated with food and tastes

A Complete the following dialogue with the phrases provided.

安　　地：孫媽媽，我來了，今天妳要
　　　　　教我做什麼菜？

孫媽媽：你＿＿＿＿＿＿＿＿＿＿＿＿＿＿
　　　　　＿＿＿＿＿＿＿＿＿＿＿＿＿＿。

安　　地：我想學中國菜，因為我不想每天吃美國菜，
　　　　　＿＿＿＿＿＿＿＿＿＿＿＿＿＿。

孫媽媽：安地，你好像＿＿＿＿＿＿＿＿。

安　　地：我好喜歡吃中國菜，我要把中國菜學好，
　　　　　這樣我就＿＿＿＿＿＿＿＿＿＿。

孫媽媽：我們先去市場買菜。

安　　地：好！

A. 可以天天都吃到中國菜
B. 而且，我的家人也喜歡中國菜
C. 可以學做中國菜，也可以學做美國菜
D. 越來越喜歡中國菜了

B In pairs, take on the roles of the two characters above and read aloud the completed dialogue. Exchange roles and repeat the exercise.

Vocabulary Builder

dàn 蛋	pí dàn 皮蛋	dàn huā tāng 蛋花湯 (egg drop soup)
dòu zi 豆子 (beans)	dòu fu 豆腐	má pó dòu fu 麻婆豆腐

suān 酸 (sour)	tián 甜 (sweet)	kǔ 苦 (bitter)
là 辣 (spicy; hot)	xián 鹹 (salty)	

yóu
油
(oil)

jiàng yóu
醬油
(soy sauce)

cù
醋
(vinegar)

hú jiāo fěn
胡椒粉
(pepper)

yán
鹽
(salt)

táng
糖
(sugar)

là jiāo
辣椒
(chili)

dà suàn
大蒜
(garlic)

cōng
蔥
(green onion)

Scrumptious Sentences

1 Discuss how the condiments and food listed above taste like.

2 Write the above vocabulary on the board and split the class into two teams.

3 The teacher randomly chooses a word. A representative from each team has to use the assigned word to form a sentence using the words on the board.

4 The team which uses more words from the board and is faster in forming the sentence wins the game.

New Words

dàn 蛋	egg
pí dàn 皮蛋	preserved egg; century egg
dòu fu 豆腐	tofu; bean curd
má pó dòu fu 麻婆豆腐	Mapo Tofu

SCENARIO: 安地 has acquired a taste for Chinese food and would like to learn to cook some Chinese dishes. One day, he calls Sunny's (以晴) mother on the phone.

　　星期六的早上，安地打電話給以晴的媽媽：「Cindy 阿姨，今天晚上我想做中國菜，可以請妳帶我去中國市場買菜嗎？」媽媽回答：「沒問題。」於是，媽媽就帶著以晴、以思和安地去中國市場買菜。

　　安地第一次去中國市場，他看到很多不一樣的東西，覺得很有趣。他拿起皮蛋問以思：「這是什麼蛋？為什麼是黑的？」以思回答：「媽媽說這種蛋叫千年蛋。千年蛋因為太老了，所以是黑的，你要不要買來吃吃看？」安地搖搖頭，說他不敢吃，他怕吃了千年蛋會生病。

　　安地又拿起圓圓的龍眼，問以晴：「這是什麼？」以思很快回答：「是 dragon's eyes，很好吃！龍眼是我最喜歡吃的水果，你要不要買一些龍眼請我

吃？」安地又搖搖頭，說他不敢吃，❶他怕吃了龍的眼睛，龍會生氣。

安地問以晴的媽媽：「Cindy阿姨，❷什麼中國菜又好吃、又容易做？」媽媽回答：「豆腐啊！豆腐好吃又便宜，又容易做，而且吃豆腐最健康。」安地聽了很高興：「真的嗎？那麼請問阿姨，豆腐可以做什麼菜？」以思說：「我知道！我知道！黑的千年蛋加上白的豆腐，好看又好吃，我也會做。」媽媽對安地說：「豆腐可以做很多菜，最有名的是麻婆豆腐。讓我教你做麻婆豆腐。」於是，他們買了做「麻婆豆腐」的東西，安地要跟Cindy阿姨學做有名的「麻婆豆腐」。

New Words

ā yí 阿姨	aunty	yú shì 於是	so; then	qiān 千	thousand
yáo tóu　yáo yáo tóu 搖頭／搖搖頭	shake head	gǎn 敢	dare	pà 怕	frighten
lóng yǎn 龍眼	longan	shuǐ guǒ 水果	fruit	lóng 龍	dragon
a 啊	ah (an exclamation)	yǒu míng 有名	well-known		

Exercises

True or False?

Answer the questions according to the passage.

　　　　　　　　　　　　　　　　　　　　　　對　　錯

1. 安地星期六早上要做中國菜。　　　　　○　　○

2. 安地想買<ruby>皮蛋<rt>pí dàn</rt></ruby>來吃吃看。　　　　○　　○

3. 安地怕<ruby>龍<rt>pà lóng</rt></ruby>生氣，所以不<ruby>敢<rt>gǎn</rt></ruby>吃<ruby>龍眼<rt>lóng yǎn</rt></ruby>。　　○　　○

4. 以思覺得<ruby>豆腐<rt>dòu fu</rt></ruby>很好吃。　　　　　　○　　○

5. <ruby>麻婆豆腐<rt>má pó dòu fu</rt></ruby>是<ruby>有名<rt>yǒu míng</rt></ruby>又容易做的中國菜。　○　　○

Think & Discuss

Work in pairs and answer the questions in Chinese.

1. 安地為什麼不<ruby>敢<rt>gǎn</rt></ruby>吃<ruby>皮蛋<rt>pí dàn</rt></ruby>和<ruby>龍眼<rt>lóng yǎn</rt></ruby>？你吃過這兩樣東西嗎？

2. 為了學做<ruby>麻婆豆腐<rt>má pó dòu fu</rt></ruby>，安地要先去市場買什麼？

3. 你去過中國市場嗎？你在那裡看到什麼？你買了什麼？

Culture Link

Preserved eggs (皮蛋 pí dàn), or century eggs, are created by covering duck eggs with preservatives such as lime, salt, and rice bran. The eggs turn black because of a biochemical reaction between the preservatives and the egg white and yolk, and not because of expiration. Preserved eggs are not harmful to one's health when eating them in moderation.

Longan's (龍眼 lóng yǎn) translucent flesh allows one to see its black pit within, giving it the appearance of an eyeball. In addition, longans were offered exclusively to the emperor in the past in China. Hence, the fruit was named "dragon's eye".

Culture Link

Names of Chinese Dishes

It is a common complaint among foreigners that the menus of Chinese restaurants are difficult to comprehend, even when the items have been translated into English. The names of Chinese dishes are often embellished, and are commonly allusive. With such names, the dishes can remain obscure to even proficient speakers of Chinese. Do you know why the tofu that Andy is learning to cook is called 麻婆 (Ma Po)?

*Sichuan (四川 sì chuān) is one of the provinces in China. Sichuan cuisine is one of the eight major schools of Chinese culinary art and is famed for its bold flavors, particularly pungency and spiciness.

Mapo tofu (麻婆豆腐) is easy to prepare and is a favorite dish among people. However, how did this traditional *Sichuan dish get its name? About 200 years ago, in the provincial capital of Sichuan, there was a restaurant. The proprietor's surname was Chen (陳), and the cook was his wife, Liu Shi (劉氏). With tofu, minced beef, chili, pepper, and bean-based sauce, Liu Shi created a dish which was delicious and popular among her customers. Word of this dish gradually got around. Liu Shi's face was pockmarked ("pockmark" is 麻子 (má zi) in Chinese), the dish was named 麻婆豆腐, literally meaning "pockmarked woman's tofu".

1

他	pà 怕	lóng 吃了龍的眼睛，	lóng 龍會生氣。
我		穿太少衣服，	很容易生病。

A: 你怎麼這麼早就要走了？

B: 我怕太晚回去，就沒有公
pà
車了。

A: 以思今天中午怎麼吃那麼多？

B: 他怕現在不吃，下午開始上
pà
課就不能吃了。

TIP The first clause after 怕 indicates some circumstances that have yet to occur and the second clause indicates the consequence of the aforementioned circumstances. This sentence implies that the subject does not wish, or is afraid to suffer the consequences. In the first example, 他 (the subject) is afraid that if he eats "dragon's eyes" (the circumstance), the dragon will be angry (the consequence).

PRACTICE IT Using sentence structure 1, complete the dialogues with the helping phrases.

1. A: 你不吃皮蛋嗎？
pí dàn

   B: _____

2. A: 你不跟我們一起去看電影嗎？

   B: _____

3. A: 你要再喝一杯茶嗎？

   B: _____

Group A	Group B
今天不看書	會生病
喝太多茶	明天的小考會考不好
吃黑色的蛋	睡覺的時候會常常想上廁所

2	什麼	中國菜	又	好吃	又	容易做？
		活動		便宜		有意思？

A: 什麼中文歌又好聽又好學？

B: 「小星星」好聽又好學。

A: 什麼比賽又有趣，又可以大家一起玩？

B: 棒球很有趣，又可以大家一起玩。

TIP "又……又……" links two attributes, conditions or situations that are deemed to be equally important by the speaker. In the first example, 又 links 好吃 and 容易做, which are both positive attributes. In essence, 又 cannot link a positive condition or attribute with a negative one.

PRACTICE IT

Based on the scenarios, create dialogues using sentence structure 2 and the helping phrases.

1. 你想看書。你問朋友……

   A: _____

   B: _____

2. 你想吃吃看不一樣的東西。你問朋友……

   A: _____

   B: _____

3. 你想養小動物。你問朋友……

   A: _____

   B: _____

Group A
便宜
可愛
故事好看

Group B
容易懂
好吃
容易照顧

Go 500 🔘 **WANT TO LEARN MORE?**

Check out the Text > Sentence Pattern section on the Go500 CD.

Listening

Go 500
Text > Dialogue section

SCENARIO: Mother is going to the market to buy groceries. She asks以思 what he would like to eat.

 A Listen to the Go500 CD for the dialogue and answer the following multiple-choice questions.

1. 媽媽說現在市場買不到什麼？

(A) 水果 *shuǐ guǒ* (B) 龍眼 *lóng yǎn* (C) 魚

2. 以思覺得什麼很可怕？

(A) 魚 (B) 龍眼 *lóng yǎn* (C) 魚眼睛

3. 誰喜歡吃有頭的魚？ *tóu*

(A) 以思 (B) 美國人 (C) 以思的媽媽

4. 為什麼以思說吃魚的時候，他是美國人的兒子？

(A) 美國人會買很多很多條魚。

(B) 以思不敢吃魚頭和魚眼睛。 *tóu*

(C) 美國的魚不會看著他，眼睛不可怕。

5. 下面哪一個是對的？

(A) 現在不是夏天。

(B) 媽媽會買有頭的魚。 *tóu*

(C) 以思看到魚眼睛會哭。

New Words

tóu 頭	head

B　Number the following texts in the correct order to form a coherent conversation.

媽媽：以思，媽媽要去中國市場買菜，你喜歡吃什麼菜？

以思：我喜歡吃魚和龍眼（lóng yǎn），可不可以＿＿＿＿＿＿魚，買＿＿＿＿＿＿＿的龍眼（lóng yǎn）？

媽媽：我覺得有頭（tóu）的魚＿＿＿＿＿＿＿！

以思：媽媽！美國人不吃魚眼睛，所以吃魚的時候，我是＿＿＿＿＿＿＿＿＿。

媽媽：為什麼？

以思：每次吃有頭（tóu）的魚，我都覺得＿＿＿＿＿＿。魚死了，眼睛很可怕，好像＿＿＿＿。

媽媽：我知道你喜歡吃魚，我會買魚。龍眼（lóng yǎn）是＿＿＿＿＿＿＿＿，現在沒有。

以思：可是，請妳不要買有頭（tóu）的魚。有頭（tóu）的魚，我＿＿＿＿。

C　Listen to the conversation on the Go500 CD again, and fill in the blanks.

Culture Link

Differences in Chinese and Western Culinary Habits

Unlike Western cuisine, where fish is often served in the form of fillets, the Chinese commonly cook fish with the tail and head intact. Some Chinese even find the fish head a delicacy. While this may seem unfeeling to some, it could be likened to the Western style of eating steak which is medium rare, or to the Japanese style of eating raw fish. It all boils down to the culinary culture of different countries.

Can you identify some food that is enjoyed by the Chinese but not Westerners? What about some food that is enjoyed by Westerners but not the Chinese?

Pair up with a classmate and role-play the following scenario. You may use the sentence structures provided below.

CHARACTERS:

張靜, 以思

SCENARIO:

During recess, 以思 sits under a tree to eat the lunch that his mother has packed for him when 張靜 goes over to say hello. 以思 does not like the fish because it was cooked with its head intact. He is afraid that he might fall ill upon eating the fish eyes. Hence, he asks 張靜 to eat it instead.

SENTENCE STRUCTURES:

1. （我）怕…… 〔pà〕
2. 什麼……又……又……？
3. ……越來越……
4. 可以……，也可以……
5. ……而且……

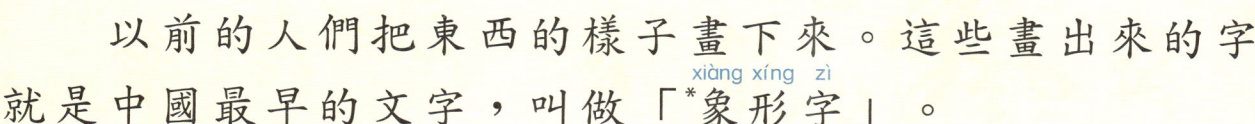

Learn about the Chinese Language & Culture

　　以前的人們把東西的樣子畫下來。這些畫出來的字就是中國最早的文字，叫做「*象形字（xiàng xíng zì）」。

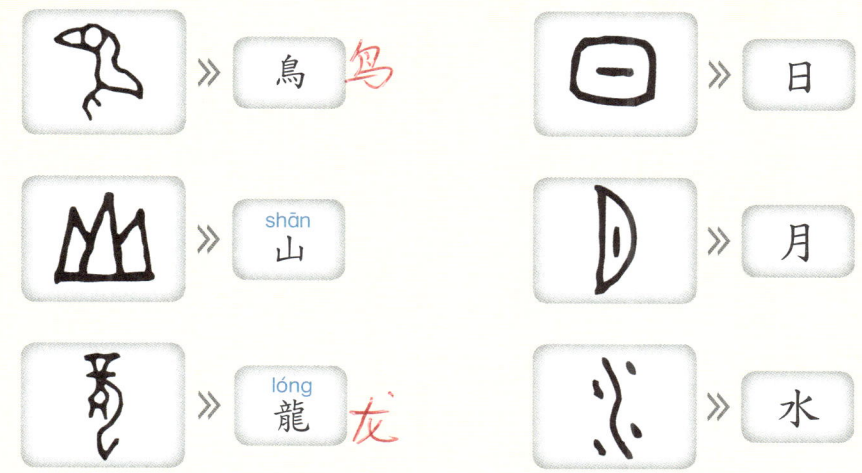

鳥　鸟

日

山（shān）

月

龍（lóng）　龙

水

　　看得到的東西可以畫出來，可是看不到的意思怎麼畫？沒問題，只要在畫出來的字的上面，再*加上（jiā shàng）一些*符（fú）號就好了。

　　我們要怎麼畫出一個東西是在「上」面，一個東西是在「下」面呢？只要先畫一條*線（xiàn），在這條線的上面或下面，再畫上一個*點（diǎn），就可以了。用這種*方法（fāng fǎ）寫出來的字，叫做「*指事字（zhǐ shì zì）」。

上

下

---

*象形字 pictographic characters　　山 hill; mountain　　加上 add　　符號 symbol　　線 line　　點 dot stroke

方法 method　　指事字 ideogram; self-explanatory characters

Work It Out

安地 has never tasted century egg and longan, but he is afraid to try them because of their names. 以思 enjoys eating fish. However, he does not like eating fish with its head intact because he is accustomed to eating fish which has been filleted. Different cultures have different culinary habits; an unpopular dish which few are willing to try in a particular culture may in fact be a delicacy in another culture.

TASK

World Delicacy Showdown

1   Get into groups of three or four. Take turns to describe a peculiar snack or dish that you have tasted or heard about. The group will vote to determine the most peculiar snack or dish.

2   In turns, each group then presents to the class the most peculiar snack or dish as discussed in the group earlier.

3   The presentation should include:

   • the country of origin, name of the dish or snack, its ingredients, and how it is prepared;

   • the taste and what is so special about it;

   • the person's feelings after consuming the dish.

LEARNING LOG

I can...

	Excellent	Good	Fair	Need Improvement
1 list the items I have purchased at the market and talk about some unusual foodstuff at the market.	○	○	○	○
2 use the sentence structure "(subject) 怕⋯⋯" to convey a consequence that the subject is afraid of or unwilling to suffer.	○	○	○	○
3 use "什麼⋯⋯ 又 (condition 1) 又 (condition 2)？" to ask for opinions.	○	○	○	○
4 identify the difference between pictographic characters and ideograms.	○	○	○	○
5 write 皮蛋, 搖頭, 阿姨, and 不敢.	○	○	○	○

誰來做家事？
Who Does the Housework?

1 What are they doing? Do you do that often?

2 Who does the housework in your family?

My Goals

1 Talk about the household chores I can do

2 Indicate that a condition needs to be satisfied before a proposition is allowed

3 Use questions to negate a proposition

4 Emphasize the fact that a situation is different from the norm

5 Understand traditional Chinese views on gender roles and housework

6 Become familiar with vocabulary related to housework

A The following pictures tell a continuous story. Number the dialogue in the correct order according to the pictures.

2　以晴：還不可以，媽媽要我把廚房打掃乾淨，才可以
　　　　出去玩。妳可以等一等嗎？

1　張靜：妳可以出來玩嗎？

3　以晴：我可以請妳幫我一起打掃廚房嗎？

4　張靜：可以，可是我怕等你打掃好了，就太晚了。

5　張靜：好啊！一起打掃比較快。

B In pairs, take on the roles of the two characters above and read aloud the dialogue in the correct order. Exchange roles and repeat the exercise.

Vocabulary Builder

cā chuāng hù
擦窗戶
(wipe the windows)

xǐ chuāng lián
洗窗簾
(wash the curtains)
帘

shuā mǎ tǒng
刷馬桶
(scrub the toilet bowl)
马

xǐ yù gāng
洗浴缸
(wash the bath tub)

pū chuáng
鋪床
(make the bed)
铺

tuō dì
拖地
(mop the floor)

sǎo dì
扫掃地
(sweep the floor)

xī dì
吸地
(vacuum the floor)

jiāo huā
澆花
(water the plants)

zhěng lǐ
整理廚房
(tidy up the kitchen)

cā liú lǐ tái
洗碗盤盘 擦梳理台
(wipe the kitchen counter)

liù gǒu
遛狗
(walk the dog)

dào lè sè
倒垃圾
(dispose of the rubbish)

cā gān
擦乾碗盤盘
干
(dry the dishes)

shōu shí
收拾碗盤盘
(clear the dishes)

幫狗洗澡

xǐ yī fú
洗衣服

tàng
烫燙衣服
(iron the laundry)

zhé
折摺衣服
(fold the laundry)

shài
曬衣服
(hang the laundry in the sun)

Interview Your Classmates

Ask three classmates about the household chores they frequently do. Do a tally of the class to determine which chores are most frequently done and which chores are least frequently done.

jiā shì
A: 你最常做的家事是什麼？

B: 我最常＿＿＿＿＿＿，我的同學常
＿＿＿＿＿＿的最多，常＿＿＿＿＿＿的
最少。

New Words

zhěng lǐ
整理 | tidy up

jiā shì
家事 | housework; household chores

SCENARIO: Andy (安地) goes to Sunny's (以晴) home to learn from her mother how to cook the famous dish, Mapo Tofu. They have a wonderful cooking experience. As the kitchen becomes very messy, Sunny's mother asks her children to clean the kitchen.

　　麻婆豆腐做好了，媽媽要以晴和以思清理廚房。以思問：「安地呢？他做什麼？」媽媽說：「安地是客人，❶怎麼可以叫客人做家事呢？」以思說：「就是因為安地要學做菜，廚房才會變得又髒又亂。他怎麼可以不做家事？」

　　媽媽說，廚房原來就髒了，不可以因為安地要學做菜，就要他幫忙整理。以晴聽了問媽媽：「可是，每次我去同學家玩，妳都叫我❷把東西收好了，才可以回家。」

　　媽媽說：「如果你們不幫忙清理，下次別人就不會歡迎你們去玩，你們一定要做一個好客人！」以晴又說：「他們家原來就是這麼亂的，我才去玩一下，為什麼要我清理呢？」以思也說：「安地也要清理，做一個好客人，下次我們才會歡迎他來玩。」

媽媽對以晴、以思說，中國人教自己的孩子要做一個好客人，可是，不能這樣對客人啊！以思聽了說：「好啊！以後我要做美國人的小孩，來媽媽的廚房做客人就好了！」

爸爸聽到他們在吵，就笑著問安地：「你覺得呢？」安地笑著說：「我當然要做一個好客人，和大家一起清理，這樣，我下次才能再請Cindy阿姨教我做菜啊！」

於是，安地和以晴、以思一起清理，廚房很快就乾乾淨淨了。安地高高興興地把麻婆豆腐拿回家請家人吃。

New Words

ne 呢	(interrogative tag used at the end of a question)	**biàn** 變	change	**shōu** 收	keep; tidy
huān yíng 歡迎	welcome	**yí dìng** 一定	definitely	**xiǎo hái** 小孩	child
dāng rán 當然	definitely				

Exercises

True or False?

Answer the questions according to the passage.

　　　　　　　　　　　　　　　　　　　　　　　　　　對　　錯

1. 以晴的媽媽覺得不能叫客人做家事_{jiā shì}。　　　✓　　○

2. 以晴的媽媽叫以晴去同學家玩，要幫忙清理　✓　　○
   以後再回家。

3. 因為安地是美國人的小孩_{xiǎo hái}，所以不用清理廚　○　　✓
   房。

4. 以晴、以思聽到安地不必幫忙整理_{zhěng lǐ}，都有一　✓　　○
   點不高興。

5. 以晴的爸爸希望安地和以晴、以思一起幫忙　✓　　○
   整理_{zhěng lǐ}。

Think & Discuss

Work in pairs and answer the questions in Chinese.

1. 以晴的媽媽覺得安地不用幫忙整理_{zhěng lǐ}廚房，可是又要
   以晴去朋友家時，一定_{yí dìng}要幫忙整理_{zhěng lǐ}。為什麼她對同
   樣的事，有不一樣的做法？

2. 你覺得去朋友家玩，要不要幫忙整理_{zhěng lǐ}？為什麼？

Culture Link

The social expectations of a host and guest vary among countries. When invited to a meal by a traditional Chinese family, the guest is not expected to help with the preparation or the cleaning up as these are the responsibilities of the host. In contrast, some Westerners enjoy preparing a meal with their guests, and everybody contributes in cleaning up after the meal.

TALK ABOUT IT

Have you ever been invited to the home of a traditional Chinese family? What are some social norms that differ from those observed in your country? Do you know of other social norms in other countries with regard to being a host and guest?

Language Focus

1 怎麼可以 ｜ 叫客人做 家事(jiā shì) ｜ 呢(ne)？
｜ 讓爺爺幫你拿書包 ｜

妹妹：姊姊，妳幫我做功課，好不好？

媽媽：怎麼可以叫姊姊幫妳做功課呢(ne)？

以思：你看，這是安地新買的書。安地不在，我先拿來看。

以晴：你怎麼可以拿別人的東西呢(ne)？

TIP This sentence structure suggests that the speaker disagrees with the proposition stated in the clause. The first example means one should not ask the guests to do the chores. In the Chinese language, questions like those above are often used to mask the negation in the proposition so that the reproach is conveyed indirectly.

PRACTICE IT

Based on the scenarios, make question sentences using sentence structure 1.

1. 你的同學在圖書館裡大聲說話，你對他們說……
   学　图书馆里　声　对　们说

   你怎么可以

2. 媽媽一進廚房，就發現廚房又髒又亂，媽媽對孩子說……
   妈　进厨　发现厨　脏乱妈妈对
   　　　　　　　　　　　　　说

   你怎么可以发现厨房又脏又乱呢？

3. 你看到弟弟打妹妹，你對弟弟說……
   　　　　　　　　　對　　說

   你怎么可以打妹妹呢？

2	把	東西收好， shōu 作業寫完，	才可以	回家。 去公園玩。

學生：我們可以下課了嗎？

老師：你們把這些句子寫完，才可以下課。

孩子：我們可以吃麵包了嗎？

媽媽：你們先把手洗乾淨，才可以吃麵包。

TIP This sentence structure suggests that only when the particular condition in the first clause is fulfilled can the proposition in the second clause be allowed. In the first example, one needs to keep his things away before he is allowed to go home. In some cases, the use of this sentence suggests that the speaker finds that it is not an easy task to fulfill the condition.

PRACTICE IT

Based on the scenarios, create dialogues using sentence structure 2 and the helping phrases.

1. 你想穿的鞋才洗好，不過還沒曬……
   shài

   A: 我現在可以穿那雙鞋了嗎？

   B: 你要先把鞋子晒于，才可以穿。 （曬乾）
   shài gān

2. 你要把洗過的碗收好……
   shōu

   A: 我可以把碗收好了吗？

   B: 你要先把洗过的碗擦干才可以收好。 （擦乾）
   cā gān

3. 現在有精彩的電影，可是明天要交作業了……

   A: 我可以看電影吗？

   B: 你要先把明天要交的作业写完才可以去看电影。 （寫完）

80　誰來做家事？

 **Listening**

Go 500

Text > Dialogue section

SCENARIO: On a weekend, 張靜 is at Sunny's (以晴) house on a play date. They happen to talk about housework.

 Listen to the Go500 CD for the dialogue and answer the following multiple-choice questions.

1. 以晴哪一天不用洗碗或整理zhěng lǐ yuàn zi院子？
   (A) 星期一　(B) 星期四　(C) 星期六

2. 以晴做jiā shì家事，媽媽會給她錢嗎？
   (A) 會　(B) 不會　(C) 不知道

3. 以晴覺得誰洗碗洗得很乾淨？
   (A) 以思　(B) 以安　(C) 安地

4. 以安和以思夏天要除草，秋天要掃落葉，冬天要劇雪，什麼時候要清理廁所？
   (A) 春天　(B) 每天　(C) 星期天

5. 下面哪一個是對的？
   (A) 以晴的媽媽會跟以晴要錢。
   (B) 張靜覺得nán hái男孩要天天清理廁所。
   (C) 以晴家的每一個xiǎo hái小孩都要做jiā shì家事。

New Words

yuàn zi 院子	courtyard	nán hái　nán hái zi 男孩／男孩子	boy
suī rán 雖然	although	dàn shì 但是	but; however

誰來做家事？　81

Number the following texts in the correct order to form a coherent conversation.

( ) 張靜：你在家裡要做家事嗎？

以晴：當然！除了整理＿＿＿＿＿＿＿＿＿，我每星期一和星期三要洗碗，星期六還要清理院子。

( ) 張靜：以安和以思他們是男孩子，也要洗碗嗎？

以晴：當然啊！男孩＿＿＿＿＿＿＿＿，為什麼男孩不用洗碗呢？你看，❸以思雖然小，雖然是男孩，但是他＿＿＿＿＿＿＿＿＿呢！

( ) 張靜：你做家事，媽媽會＿＿＿＿＿＿嗎？

以晴：為什麼要給錢？如果我做家事跟媽媽要錢，媽媽也會跟我要錢。＿＿＿＿＿＿＿＿一定比我多，我給她的錢，一定會比＿＿＿＿＿＿＿＿多。

( ) 張靜：我是說，女孩可以洗碗，男孩可以做其他的家事啊！

以晴：對！男孩可以＿＿＿＿＿除草，＿＿＿＿＿掃落葉，＿＿＿＿＿剷雪，還要他們＿＿＿＿＿清理廁所。

C Listen to the conversation on the Go500 CD again, and fill in the blanks.

3

以思 雖然 _{suī rán} 小，	但是 _{dàn shì} 他洗碗洗得很乾淨。
中文書很貴，	我還是買了兩本。

A: 你的中文說得很好，還要來上課嗎？

B: 我_{suī rán}雖然會說中文，_{dàn shì}但是說得還不夠好。

A: 以思說他每天都要倒垃圾_{dào lè sè}，你也要一起幫忙嗎？

B: 我_{suī rán}雖然不用倒垃圾_{dào lè sè}，_{dàn shì}但是我每天都要掃地_{sǎo dì}、拖地_{tuō dì}。

TIP In this sentence structure, the first clause conveys a fact. The second clause states something contrary to one's expectations with regard to the aforementioned fact. In the first example, the speaker acknowledges the fact that 以思 is a young kid and implies that young kids generally do not wash the dishes well. However, the truth is contrary to the implied expectation. Hence, 但是 (but) is used as a contrasting connector to convey that 以思 can in fact wash the dishes well. Also, the subject can be positioned either before or after the word 雖然.

PRACTICE IT

Using sentence structure 3, rewrite the sentences with the helping phrases.

1. 哥哥坐公車上學只要二十分鐘，可是他想走路。

_____

2. 今天老師沒來，大家都在玩，只有他在做功課。

_____

Group A
老師不在
每天都很忙
坐公車很方便

Group B
天天做運動
想走路去
認真做功課

3. 叔叔每天有很多事要做，他還是每天慢跑。

_____

Role Playing

Form groups of four and role-play the scenario. You may use the sentence structures provided below.

CHARACTERS:

孫媽媽，以思，以晴，以安

SCENARIO:

以思 is washing the dishes in the kitchen when there is a loud crash. Everybody rushes into the kitchen and 以安 blames 以思 for breaking one of Mother's favorite bowls. This upsets 以思. However, Mother and 以晴 feel that it is an accident and 以安 should not blame 以思.

SENTENCE STRUCTURES:

1. 怎麼可以……呢 (ne)？

2. 把……，才可以……

3. 雖然 (suī rán)……，但是 (dàn shì)……

4. 什麼……又……又……？

Culture Link

Traditionally, the Chinese have very fixed gender roles. As the males were typically the sole breadwinners in the past, it was imperative that they were well educated so they could secure a good job. On the other hand, the females were typically homemakers who were expected to handle all kinds of household chores. Hence, the boys were commonly excused from household chores, unlike the girls. These gender roles are reflected in the characters: 男 is made up of 田 (tián, field) and 力 (lì, strength), suggesting that males are the ones who work in the fields to support their families; the character 女 reflects a female kneeling on the ground and cradling a baby, suggesting that it is a female's responsibility to take care of her family at home.

TALK ABOUT IT

What are your views on such gender roles? How do these gender roles differ from those in your country? Interview your family and friends to get their views on gender roles.

84   誰來做家事？

Learn about the Chinese Language & Culture

你知道為什麼華人吃*年夜飯（nián yè fàn）的時候桌上要有魚嗎？

「魚」讀「yú」，「*餘（yú）」也讀「yú」，這兩個字的*發音（fā yīn）一樣。「餘」是「剩下（shèng xià）」的意思，*以前（yǐ qián）的人希望東西可以用不完、吃不完。今天吃不完的東西，可以明天吃；今年用不完的東西，可以明年用。

希望每年有用不完的東西給第二年用，所以吃年（nián）夜飯（yè fàn）的時候，就在桌上放一條魚，「年年有魚」就像是「年年有餘（yú）」一樣。

除了魚，*年糕（nián gāo）也是一樣的。

「糕」讀「gāo」，你一定（yí dìng）想到了，這和你學過的「高」發音（fā yīn）一樣，吃「年糕（nián gāo）」就是希望小孩可以「年年長高」，*大人（dà rén）的工作*職位（zhí wèi）也一年比一年高。

「有魚」、「有餘（yú）」；「年糕（nián gāo）」、「年高」，這種除了原來的意思外，還有另一種意思的*詞（cí）或句子，就是「*雙關語（shuāng guān yǔ）」。在寫句子或說話的時候，用雙關語（shuāng guān yǔ）會讓句子更有趣。

*年夜飯 reunion dinner　　餘 surplus　　發音 pronunciation　　剩下 remaining　　以前 in the past

年糕 glutinous rice cake (usually eaten during Lunar New Year)　　大人 adult　　職位 (job) post

詞 phrase　　雙關語 pun

Work It Out

When you have many household chores to complete, the ones you enjoy will be a breeze while the ones you dislike will be tedious.

TASK

My Daily Chore

1   Choose a household chore from the list below.

2   Take a few photographs of yourself performing that chore. Alternatively, record it on video.

3   Create a bulletin from the pictures by tagging and explaining each picture according to the following points.

   • The time this chore is performed.   • Whether or not you like it and why.
   • Things to note.   • Tips on how to do the chore well.

4   Present your bulletin to the class.

Household chore

pū chuáng	sǎo dì	xī dì	tuō dì		dào lè sè
鋪床	掃地	吸地	拖地	洗碗	倒垃圾

bǎi cān jù		tàng	shài	zhé	shuā mǎ tǒng
擺餐具 (set the table)	洗衣服	燙衣服	曬衣服	摺衣服	刷馬桶

xǐ yù gāng	xiū shuǐ guǎn	jiāo huā		cā chuāng hù	jiǎn zhé jià quàn
洗浴缸	修水管 (repair the water pipe)	澆花	除草	擦窗戶	剪折價券 (cut out discount coupons)

洗車	鏟雪	liù gǒu 遛狗	幫狗洗澡		

LEARNING LOG

I can...

		Excellent	Good	Fair	Need Improvement
1	state and give reasons for the household chores I like and dislike.	○	○	○	○
2	use the sentence structure "怎麼可以……呢？" and "把……，才可以……" to form sentences.	○	○	○	○
3	use the sentence structure "雖然……，但是……" to indicate that a situation is different from the norm.	○	○	○	○
4	explain how the characters 男 and 女 were formed from traditional gender roles.	○	○	○	○
5	write 當然, 雖然, 但是, and 歡迎.	○	○	○	○

廚房安全
Safety in the kitchen

My Goals

1 Identify household risks and suggest ways to make the home safer
2 Make suggestions tactfully
3 Rebut a proposition using a negative question
4 Understand the origins of picto-phonetic characters and associative compound characters
5 Become familiar with vocabulary associated with cooking and kitchen appliances

1 What is wrong with this kitchen?
2 What accidents might happen?

SCENARIO: 以思 tells 安地 that his mother will let him try cooking in the kitchen next Sunday.

A Complete the following dialogue by choosing the correct options listed below.

以思：安地，從下個星期起，我跟你一樣可以在廚房做菜了。

安地：你才五年級，＿＿＿＿＿＿＿＿＿＿＿＿＿＿

以思：為什麼不可以？＿＿＿＿＿＿＿＿＿＿＿

安地：你在廚房做過東西了嗎？

以思：還沒有，＿＿＿＿＿＿＿＿＿

＿＿＿＿＿＿＿＿＿＿＿＿＿＿＿＿

安地：＿＿＿＿＿＿＿以後我們可以一起做中國菜。

以思：好啊！

A. 雖然我才十歲，但是我也可以做菜。

B. 以晴和以安給我上過課以後，我就能開始用了。

C. 太好了！

D. 你做的菜怎麼樣？

E. 怎麼可以在廚房做菜？

B In pairs, take on the roles of the two characters above and read aloud the completed dialogue. Exchange roles and repeat the exercise.

Vocabulary Builder

diàn guō	shuǐ hú	guō zi	shuǐ lóng tóu	wǎ sī lú
電鍋	水壺	鍋子	水龍頭	瓦斯爐
(rice cooker)	(kettle)	(pot)	(tap)	(gas stove)

wéi bō lú	kǎo xiāng	bīng xiāng	cài dāo	qiē cài bǎn
微波爐	烤箱	冰箱	菜刀	切菜板
(microwave oven)	(oven)	(refrigerator)	(knife)	(chopping block)

wéi xiǎn	shòu shāng	huá dǎo	tàng shāng
危險	受傷	滑倒	燙傷
(dangerous)	(injured)	(slip and fall)	(scald)

qiē	dào shuǐ	chù diàn	shī huǒ
切	倒(水)	觸電	失火
(cut)	(pour (water))	(electric shock)	(catch fire)

kāi huǒ	guān huǒ	jiā rè	jiān	zhǔ
開火	關火	加熱	煎	煮
(turn on the fire (of stove))	(turn off the fire)	(heat)	(pan fry)	(cook)

zhēng	dùn	chǎo	zhá	kǎo
蒸	燉	炒	炸	烤
(steam)	(stew)	(stir-fry)	(deep-fry)	(roast)

Charades Face-off

1 Divide into Team A and Team B for a game of charades. When a player is acting out a word, either team can answer.

2 A team gets one point if it correctly guesses the word acted out by its team member and 1.5 points if it intercepts and correctly guesses the word acted out by an opposing member.

3 Once everybody in the teams has acted out a word, the team with the higher score wins.

New Words

guān huǒ 關火	turn off the fire (of stove)

廚房安全

SCENARIO: 以思 can finally prepare food for himself in the kitchen, just like his brother and sister. However, 以思 must take note of a few things before using the kitchen.

在以晴家，星期日是媽媽休息的日子。爸爸說，媽媽從星期一到星期六，每天做飯很辛苦，星期日這一天，媽媽不用做飯。以前，除了最小的以思，大家想吃什麼，就自己動手做。從今年九月開始，❶以思已經十歲，上五年級了，爸爸和媽媽也讓他做自己喜歡吃的東西。

媽媽對大家說：「從明天起，以思可以在廚房做自己喜歡吃的東西了，❷讓我們幫以思上第一節課吧！」於是，媽媽拿了一張紙給以思，要以思把大家說的話都寫在紙上。以思寫的是：

一、做菜前，要洗手。

二、洗菜時，洗乾淨。

三、用刀子，要小心。

四、用火時，要注意。

五、做菜時，要用心。

六、做完菜，先關火。

七、做好菜，要清理。

八、用熱水，要小心。

九、吃完飯，要洗碗。

十、離開前，檢查火。

寫完後，以思對媽媽說：「吃飯很容易，做飯真難！吃飯只要十分鐘，做飯卻要一小時。我希望我們星期日常常不在家。」以晴說：「沒關係！不用怕！以後的星期日，我們一起做飯，我們一起清理，大家一起做，大家一起吃，一點也不難！」

New Words

rì zi 日子 | day	yǐ jīng 已經 | already	jié 節 | session	ba 吧 | (exclamation tag)
huǒ 火 | fire	rè shuǐ 熱水 | hot water	lí kāi 離開 | leave	jiǎn chá 檢查 | check

Exercises

Answer the questions according to the passage.

對　錯

1. 在以晴家，星期天大家常常不在家。　○　⊘

2. 以思五年級以前不能自己進廚房做菜。　⊗　○

3. 媽媽幫以思把大家說的話寫在紙上。　✓　○

4. 以思覺得做菜很不容易。　✓　○

5. 星期六，為了教以思用廚房，大家幫他上 第一節課。　✓　○

Think & Discuss

Work in pairs and answer the questions in Chinese.

1. 以思學怎麼在廚房做菜的第一節^{jié}課，學的是什麼？

2. 如果請你幫以思上課，你會教他什麼？

3. 你也可以在廚房做自己喜歡吃的東西嗎？從什麼 時候開始的？你在廚房有什麼難忘的事嗎？

1

以思	yǐ jīng 已經	十歲	了。
媽媽		做好飯	

以晴 yǐ jīng 已經會說中文了。

以思 yǐ jīng 已經把院子整理好了。

TIP This sentence structure suggests that an action or event is over, or that a situation or state of affairs has changed. The first example, 以思已經十歲了, shows that a state of affairs has changed — 以思 just turned ten. The second example indicates that an action is completed — Mother was still cooking some time ago but she has finished cooking now.

PRACTICE IT

Using sentence structure 1, complete the dialogues.

1. A: 你 guān huǒ 關火了嗎？

   B: _____

2. A: 廚房清理乾淨了嗎？

   B: _____

3. A: 小明說，上個星期六你媽媽教他做中國菜。

   B: 是啊！_____

2	讓	我們	幫以思上第一節^{jié}課	吧^{ba}！
		大家	幫哥哥清理廚房	

A: 讓我們跟新同學介紹自己吧^{ba}！

B: 好啊！

A: 讓我來幫你吧^{ba}！

B: 謝謝！

TIP
吧 is used at the end of an imperative so that the suggestion is less forceful and more tactful.

PRACTICE IT

Based on the scenarios, make sentences using sentence structure 2.

1. 你看到教室很髒，你對你的朋友說……

_____

2. 安地學會做麻婆豆腐了，他想請大家吃，他對
大家說……

_____

3. 班上來了一個新同學，你對他說……

_____

Go500 **WANT TO LEARN MORE?**
Check out the Text > Sentence Pattern section on the Go500 CD.

Listening

Go 500
Text > Dialogue section

SCENARIO: It is the first time 以思 cooks something in the kitchen.

A Listen to the Go500 CD for the dialogue and answer the following multiple-choice questions. Question 5 may have more than one answer.

1. 做菜前，以思洗手了嗎？
    (A) 洗了　(B) 沒洗　(C) 不知道

2. 為什麼以思沒洗碗？
    (A) 他忘記了　(B) 他要先休息一下　(C) 他還要用

3. 為什麼以思一做飯，大家就對他說不停？
    (A) 以思不會做飯。
    (B) 大家怕以思做不好。
    (C) 大家不想吃以思做的飯。

4. 以思聽到大家的問題，覺得怎麼樣？
    (A) 做飯真難　(B) 不開心　(C) 很累

5. 以思第一次做菜的時候，以晴和以安看到什麼？
    (A) 以思離開廚房沒關火。
    (B) 以思的手髒髒的。
    (C) 以思在洗碗。
    (D) 以思的飯已經做好了。
    (E) 以思沒有收東西。
    (F) 廚房又髒又亂。

Number the following texts in the correct order to form a coherent conversation.

（　　）以晴：以思，你忘了洗碗！也＿＿＿＿收東西，
　　　　　　　廚房又髒又亂。
　　　　以思：我＿＿＿＿＿＿！我累了，我要先休息一下！

（　　）以安：以思，你忘記＿＿＿＿了，離開前一定要
　　　　　　　lí kāi
　　　　　　　＿＿＿＿！
　　　　以思：我沒有忘！我要去上廁所！

（　　）以晴：以思，做菜前，＿＿＿＿＿＿＿＿＿＿？
　　　　以思：我有，❸ 我洗菜的時候，＿＿＿＿＿＿
　　　　　　　＿＿＿＿？你看，我的
　　　　　　　手多乾淨啊！

（　　）以安：你的刀子＿＿＿＿
　　　　　　　＿＿？怎麼沒有收好？
　　　　　　　怎麼丟在這裡？
　　　　以思：我＿＿＿＿＿＿！我的天！你們做飯的
　　　　　　　時候，我都沒有說話，為什麼我一做飯，
　　　　　　　你們就＿＿＿＿＿！

Listen to the conversation on the Go500 CD again, and fill in the blanks.

Language Focus

3

我洗菜	的時候，（我）不是	在洗手	嗎？
昨天下課		把書拿給你了	

A: 我做飯的時候，你都不來幫忙。

B: 你做飯的時候，我不是幫你洗菜了嗎？

A: 昨天電視介紹的電影，你想去看嗎？

B: 星期天哥哥生日的時候，我們不是要一起去看嗎？

> **TIP** The first phrase provides the listener with the time frame in which the action in the second phrase occurred. The rebuttal in the second phrase is veiled by the negative question "不是……嗎？" When the subject of the first and second clauses is the same, the subject can be omitted in either clause.

 **PRACTISE IT**

Using sentence structure 3, complete the dialogues with the helping phrases.

1. A: 你關火了嗎？
   <small>guān huǒ</small>

   B: 關了，_____
   <small>guān</small>

   _____

2. A: 雖然才吃過晚飯，可是我肚子又餓了！

   B: 你又餓了！_____

   _____

3. A: 龍眼是什麼？我吃過嗎？

   B: _____

Group A

去中國市場

吃晚飯

離開廚房
<small>lí kāi</small>

Group B

檢查
<small>jiǎn chá</small>

吃過了

吃了很多

Go 500 **WANT TO LEARN MORE?**

Check out the Text > Sentence Pattern section on the Go500 CD.

Culture Link

In the previous lesson, we discussed the meaning behind the character "男". Men were expected to go out to work to support their families while the kitchen was the women's domain. However, times have changed. Many mothers in modern families work to support the family too, and some meals are prepared by fathers instead. Besides, the chefs of many restaurants are also men. As such, such fixed gender roles seem to be outmoded.

1 Do the males in your family (father or brother) prepare meals?

2 Does the society you live in hold the view that men should not cook or perform household chores? What are your views on this subject?

Role Playing

Form groups of four and role-play the scenario. You may use the sentence structures provided below.

CHARACTERS:

安地, 以思, 以晴, 以安

SCENARIO:

以思 has invited 安地 to his house to cook some tofu dishes together. 以晴 and 以安 helped to buy the ingredients the day before and they join in the cooking session as well.

SENTENCE STRUCTURES:

yǐ jīng
1. 已經……了

　　bɑ
2. 讓……吧！

3. ……的時候，（我）不是……嗎？

4. 雖然……，但是……

5. 怎麼可以……呢？

Learn about the
Chinese Language & Culture

以前的人用「*象形（xiàng xíng）」、「*指事（zhǐ shì）」畫出很多字，可是，大家很快就覺得字不夠用了。如果想要用字把大家的想法記下來，要想想別的*方法（fāng fǎ）才行。於是，有人想出了把兩個畫出來的字放在一起的方法（fāng fǎ），兩個不一樣的字放在一起，就變成了新的字。

把兩個或更多的字放在一起，*表示（biǎo shì）一個新的意思，就是「*會意字（huì yì zì）」。看看下面兩個字：

「雙」是手上*抓（zhuā）著兩隻小鳥。

「看」是一個人把手放在眼睛*上方（shàng fāng），可以看得*遠（yuǎn）。

把兩個字放在一起，一個表示（biǎo shì）意思，一個表示（biǎo shì）*聲音（shēng yīn），就叫做「*形聲字（xíng shēng zì）」。

這些我們學過的字都是形聲字（xíng shēng zì）：

有了這兩種新的*方法（fāng fǎ）後，就有更多的文字了。

---

*象形(字) pictographic characters　　指事(字) self-explanatory characters　　方法 method　　表示 symbolize

會意字 associative compound characters　　抓 grab　　上方 above　　遠 far　　聲音 sound

形聲字 picto-phonetic characters

TASK

Identify Danger Zone to Keep Your Family Safe

1 Discuss in teams which areas at home are prone to accident and identify specific areas that are dangerous. List these areas in order, starting with the most dangerous area. For example: Bathroom → Kitchen → Living room…

2 Write down the reason you think these areas are so dangerous. For example: Bathroom – one may slip easily; the pipes may burst…

3 Think about appliances that require the use of fire, electricity, water, and gas. Can you think of ways to make the use of such appliances safer? For example, think about some safety precautions that can be taken? Are there parts that need to be checked?

4 After the discussion, create a letter size or A4-sized poster with your notes and paste it at home.

LEARNING LOG

I can...

		Excellent	Good	Fair	Need Improvement
1	identify accidents that commonly happen at home and suggest safety precautions.	○	○	○	○
2	use "讓⋯⋯吧！" to make a suggestion less forceful.	○	○	○	○
3	use "⋯⋯的時候，(我) 不是⋯⋯嗎？" to indicate that the speaker disagrees with what the listener previously mentioned.	○	○	○	○
4	use the sentence structures "已經⋯⋯了" to form sentences.	○	○	○	○
5	state the differences between picto-phonetic characters and associative compound characters.	○	○	○	○
6	write 關火, 熱水, 離開, and 檢查.	○	○	○	○

我的學校
My School

My Goals

1 Introduce my school and my community
2 Describe various aspects of a particular scenario
3 State the reason for a particular outcome
4 Use contrasting concepts to highlight something that is important
5 Identify the ways the Chinese usher in good luck and fortune
6 Become familiar with vocabulary associated with a school campus

1 What scenes do these pictures portray?
2 What are these students doing?

Get Started

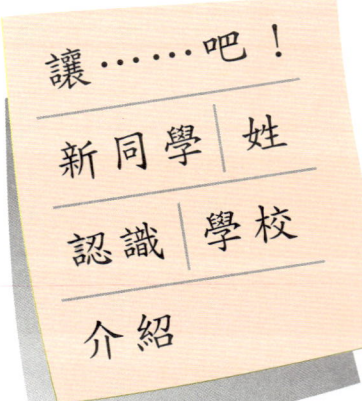

讓……吧！

新同學 ｜ 姓
認識 ｜ 學校
介紹

今天上課的時候，_____

_____

_____

下課的時候，我對她說：_____

_____

_____

大家都很喜歡新同學，_____

_____

_____

B Read your completed sentences aloud to your partner.

Vocabulary Builder

huán jìng
環境
(environment; surroundings)

xiào yuán
校園

cān guān
參觀

zǒu láng
走廊
(corridor)

liáo tiān
聊天
(chat)

tiē
貼

liú huà
留話

guì zi
櫃子

xiào chē
校車
(school bus)

yì pái
一排

pái duì
排隊

bāng zhù
幫助
(help)

xuǎn kè
選課
(choose a course)

zuò shí yàn
做實驗
(do an experiment)

fēn zǔ
分組
(divide into groups)

xiǎo zǔ tǎo lùn
小組討論
(group discussion)

Memory Jolt and Bolt

1 Memorize the above vocabulary and then close the book.

2 Divide into two teams. In turn, each team sends a representative to the board to write a word he or she has memorized. The words should not be repeated.

3 Later, the teacher selects a word and reverses the order of the characters, e.g. 助幫. Both teams send a representative each to identify the word in the correct order e.g. 幫助.

4 The team whose representative circles the word on the board first wins one point. The team with the highest score wins the game.

New Words

xiào yuán 校園	campus	liú huà 留話	leave a message
cān guān 參觀	visit	tiē 貼	paste
guì zi 櫃子	locker	pái duì 排隊	queue up
pái ……排	row		

SCENARIO: During class, the teacher introduces a new student to everybody.

今天，老師給大家介紹一位新同學，他的名字叫方健。方健來美國才三個月，英文不太好。老師問：「誰會說中文？誰<ruby>願意<rt>yuàn yì</rt></ruby>下課後帶方健看一看我們的<ruby>校園<rt>xiào yuán</rt></ruby>？」以晴說：「我會說中文，我<ruby>願意<rt>yuàn yì</rt></ruby>帶方健認識一下我們的學校。」

下課後，以晴帶方健<ruby>參觀<rt>cān guān</rt></ruby>了學校，見到了校長，還有老師。這個學校只有三<ruby>排<rt>pái</rt></ruby>教室，五百多個學生。方健對以晴說：「這個學校真小！教室小，老師少，學生也少。妳知道嗎？我原來的學校有三千多個學生呢！」以晴說：「**1** 學校小、學生少，這樣，老師才能認識每一個學生；還有買<ruby>午飯<rt>wǔ fàn</rt></ruby>、參加活動的時候，也不用<ruby>排<rt>pái</rt></ruby>長長的<ruby>隊<rt>duì</rt></ruby>啊！」

方健看到每一間教室外面都有一<ruby>排<rt>pái</rt></ruby>長長的<ruby>櫃<rt>guì</rt></ruby><ruby>子<rt>zi</rt></ruby>，就問以晴為什麼。以晴說：「每個學生都有自己的<ruby>櫃子<rt>guì zi</rt></ruby>，可以放書包、<ruby>鞋子<rt>xié zi</rt></ruby>，還有其他的東西。最重要的是，我們可以在<ruby>櫃子<rt>guì zi</rt></ruby>上<ruby>留話<rt>liú huà</rt></ruby>。」於是，以

晴帶方健去看久美子的櫃子（guì zi）。久美子❷櫃子（guì zi）的門上有很多留話（liú huà），有的是用英文寫的，有的是用日文寫的，還有一句用中文寫的「生日快樂」。

以晴問方健的櫃子（guì zi）在哪裡，她拿了一張紙，在上面用中文和英文寫了「歡迎」兩個字，貼（tiē）在方健的櫃子（guì zi）上。方健看了很開心，也在紙上寫了一個「吉」（jí）字。以晴問他是什麼意思？方健說：「新開的商店（shāng diàn）常常會在大門（dà mén）上寫上『吉』（jí）這個字，希望大吉大利（dà jí dà lì），運氣好。來到新學校，我當然希望我的運氣也會好啊！」以晴聽了覺得很有趣，就把「吉」（jí）這個字倒過來（dào guò lái），對方健說：「希望你的『吉』（jí）到了！」

New Words

願意（yuàn yì）	willing	午飯（wǔ fàn）	lunch
鞋子（xié zi）	shoes	吉（jí）	lucky; auspicious
商店（shāng diàn）	store	大門（dà mén）	gate; main entrance
大吉大利（dà jí dà lì）	good luck and good fortune		
倒（dào）/ 倒過來（dào guò lái）	upside down		

Exercises

True or False?

Answer the questions according to the passage.

對　錯

1. 以晴的英文很好，所以願意帶方健參觀學校。　○　○
yuàn yì　cān guān

2. 以晴覺得學校小也很好。　○　○

3. 每一間教室外面都有一排櫃子，是讓學生留話用的。　○　○
pái guì zi　liú　huà

4. 以晴不認識「吉」這個字，所以把這個字倒過來。　○　○
jí　dào　guò lái

5. 方健開了一家商店，所以他要在櫃子上貼「吉」。　○　○
shāng diàn　guì zi tiē jí

Think & Discuss

Work in pairs and answer the questions in Chinese.

1. 方健原來的學校大，還是現在的學校大？你喜歡大的學校，還是小的學校？為什麼？

2. 你都怎麼給同學留話？看下面的句子，把你的留話寫下來。
liú huà　liú huà

1. Your classmate has just returned from a holiday in Japan. Ask him or her about the trip.

2. Remind your friend about a ball game at 6 pm.

3. You have learned to cook some Chinese dishes and would like to cook a meal for your friend. Ask when he or she is free.

Language Focus

1

學校小、學生少，	這樣，
明天你可以早一點來，	這樣，

老師	才	能認識每一個學生。
我們		可以多玩一下。

A: 什麼活動大家都會來參加？
B: 活動要安全、有意思，
   這樣，大家才會想參加。

A: 我的中文學不好，怎麼辦？
B: 你要多說、多聽、多看，
   這樣，中文才學得好。

TIP In this sentence structure, the clause before 這樣 conveys a reason while the clause after 才 conveys the result. In the first example, the teacher knows every student (result) because the school and student population are small (reason).

 **PRACTICE IT**

Based on the scenarios, make sentences using sentence structure 1 and the helping phrases.

1. 你的同學生病兩個星期都還沒有好。你對同學說……

_____

2. 舅舅新開了一家店，卻很少人來買東西。他的朋友對他說……

_____

Group A	Group B	Group C
東西好又便宜	病	會更想買
多喝水，多休息	大家	會快點好

2

| 櫃子的門上有很多留話， | 有的 | 是用英文寫的， |
| 我和朋友一起做菜， | | 做中國菜， |

| 有的 | 是用日文寫的， | 還有 | 一句用中文寫的。 |
| | 做日本菜， | | 做印度菜的。 |

A: 下課的時候，大家會做什麼？
B: 大家做的事都不一樣，有的休息，有的跟朋友說話，還有人吃東西。

TIP In this sentence structure, the first clause provides a general description about a situation or a scene. The clauses that follow 有的 state specific and different details. The particular detail that is exceptional is placed after 還有 for emphasis.

A: 你的同學都是美國人嗎？
B: 不是，很多同學從不同的國家來，有的是日本人，有的是英國人，還有的是中國人。

PRACTICE IT

Using sentence structure 2, complete the dialogues with the helping phrases.

1. A: 這家書店的書多嗎？

   B: _____

2. A: 從這裡去機場只能坐計程車嗎？

   B: _____

| 雜誌 | 小說 | 火車 |
| 地鐵 | 公車 | 故事書 |

Listening

Go 500

Text > Dialogue section

SCENARIO: After school, 以晴 visits her friend, 白爺爺.
They talk about how 以晴 feels about her new school.

A Listen to the Go500 CD for the dialogue and answer the following multiple-choice questions. Question 4 may have more than one answer.

1. 以晴覺得新學校怎麼樣？
 (A) 在不同的教室上課，很有趣。
 (B) 大家都在同樣的教室上課，一起學不同的學科。
 (C) 參加新學校的活動很忙，但是很開心。

2. 以晴不喜歡新學校什麼事？
 (A) 在不一樣的教室上課，每天要跑來跑去。
 (B) 學校有很多活動，每天都很忙。
 (C) 老師給太多功課，沒時間找白爺爺。

3. 以晴想教白爺爺什麼？
 (A) 課外活動 (B) 說中文 (C) 玩電腦遊戲

4. 以晴喜歡新學校的什麼？

 (A)  (B)  (C)  (D)

5. 下面哪一個是對的？
 (A) 白爺爺不喜歡以晴的新學校。
 (B) 白爺爺覺得在不同的教室上課很有趣。
 (C) 白爺爺希望以晴不要交新朋友，這樣，才不會忘了他這個老朋友。

New Words

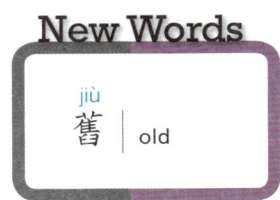

jiù
舊 | old

B Number the following texts in the correct order to form a coherent conversation.

〇 白爺爺：妳不喜歡新學校的什麼呢？

以　晴：以前除了體育課和課外活動，大家都在＿＿＿＿＿＿＿＿上課，一起學不同的學科，不用跑來跑去。現在，每一個人選的課不一樣，不同的學科要去不同的教室，跑來跑去找教室，很辛苦。

- -

〇 白爺爺：＿＿＿＿了新朋友，＿＿＿＿＿＿＿＿舊^{jiù}朋友，還有白爺爺這個「老」朋友啊！

以　晴：＿＿＿＿＿＿＿＿！以後我可以教白爺爺玩更多好玩的電腦遊戲了。

- -

〇 白爺爺：以晴，妳喜歡妳的新學校嗎？

以　晴：＿＿＿＿＿＿喜歡，＿＿＿＿＿＿不喜歡。

- -

〇 白爺爺：在不同的教室上課，不是很有趣嗎？那麼妳喜歡新學校的什麼呢？

以　晴：新學校有很多有趣的＿＿＿＿＿＿：除了唱歌、跳舞、打球和參加樂隊活動，還可以玩數學遊戲和電腦遊戲。我每天有不同的課外活動，認識了很多新朋友。❸雖然＿＿＿＿，可是＿＿＿＿＿＿＿＿＿＿。

C Listen to the conversation on the Go500 CD again, and fill in the blanks.

110　我的學校

3	雖然	很忙，	可是	很開心。
		不便宜，		很好用。

A: 學中文很難嗎？

B: 雖然有點難，可是很有趣。

A: 這雙鞋很好看！

B: 雖然好看，可是太貴了。

TIP This sentence structure is used to balance two opposing attributes or sentiments. In the first example, although the speaker is very busy (a negative sentiment), he is nonetheless happy (a positive sentiment). These two opposing sentiments are thus connected by 可是 (but). This is similar to the sentence structure "雖然……，但是……" we learned in Lesson 6.

PRACTICE IT

Based on the scenarios, make sentences using sentence structure 3 and the helping phrases.

1. 你看到一隻很可愛的小狗，你想帶回家。
你爸爸說……

_____

2. 你的同學想找你出去玩，但是你還沒有
寫完作業。你對朋友說……

_____

3. 老師給了今天的作業，他對學生說……

_____

Group A

想去

可愛

不多

Group B

不容易做

還沒寫完

不能養

Check out the Text > Sentence Pattern section on the Go500 CD.

Upon moving to a new place or opening a new shop, it is customary for the Chinese to do something auspicious like lighting fire crackers or writing characters such as 福 (fortune), 財 (cái wealth), or 吉 (jí luck) on red paper and hanging them upside down (倒 dào) on the wall or door. Hanging these characters upside down is believed to bring about the arrival (到 dào) of luck and prosperity.

1 In your country, what do people do for good luck?

2 Can you guess why the acts in these pictures are believed to bring good luck?

Role Playing

Pair up and role-play the scenario. You may use the sentence structures provided below.

CHARACTERS:

以晴, 方健

SCENARIO:

With Sunny's (以晴) help, 方健 has adapted very well to his school despite being new to the environment. Today, he is going to choose his co-curricular activities and he asks 以晴 to tell him more about the co-curricular activities offered.

SENTENCE STRUCTURES:

1. 有的⋯⋯，有的⋯⋯，還有⋯⋯

2. ⋯⋯，這樣，⋯⋯才能⋯⋯

3. 雖然⋯⋯，可是⋯⋯

4. 可以⋯⋯嗎？

Learn about the
Chinese Language & Culture

以晴在方健的櫃子（guì zi）上貼（tiē）了「歡迎」，方健也給自己貼（tiē）了一個「吉（jí）」字。

中國人喜歡把*吉利話（jí lì huà）寫在紅紙上，再把這張紅紙貼在（tiē）*牆上（qiáng）或門上（mén）。

這些吉利話（jí lì huà）有的只有一個字，像是「春」、「福」，有的兩個字，像是「大吉（dà jí）」，還有四個字的，像是「大吉大利（dà jí dà lì）」、「春回大地」。

有時大家會把寫好的吉利字（jí lì）倒過來貼（dào guò lái tiē）。把「福」倒（dào）過來貼（guò lái tiē），是希望運氣、*福氣（fú qì）「到來」；把「春」倒過（dào guò）來（lái），是說「春到了」。

還有一種是把四個字的吉利話（jí lì huà）寫在一起，像是：

日日有*財（cái）

（每天都有錢）

*招財進（zhāo cái）*寶（bǎo）

（把錢和*寶物（bǎo wù）帶回家）

---

*吉利話 greetings of luck and fortune　　牆 wall　　福氣 good fortune　　財 money　　招 bring in
寶／寶物 treasure

Work It Out

Your neighbor is new to the neighborhood. How can you help him or her get to know the area better? What are some key features of the neighborhood that he or she needs to know?

TASK

Construct a Map of the Neighborhood to Help Your Neighbor Get Around

1. Form small groups, preferably with classmates who live in the same area.
2. List the areas in the neighborhood that are important, or are relevant to one's daily life (e.g. hospital, supermarket, park, basketball court).
3. List some unique and important aspects of the neighborhood that your new neighbor needs to know to better integrate into the area.
4. Construct a map of your neighborhood based on the points discussed.
5. Make a video introducing various areas of the neighborhood and some activities to be carried out there.

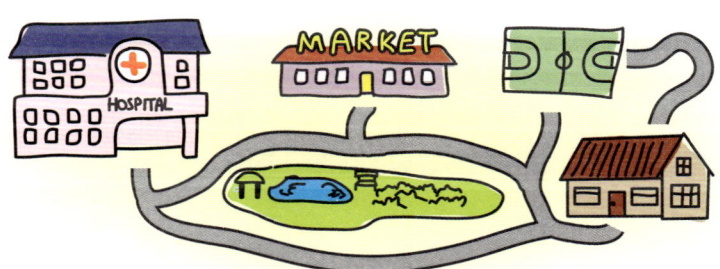

LEARNING LOG

I can...

	Excellent	Good	Fair	Need Improvement
1 introduce the surroundings to my new classmates or neighbor.	○	○	○	○
2 use "······，這樣，······才······" to convey a reason and a corresponding result.	○	○	○	○
3 use "有的······，有的······，還有······" to describe different details which are part of a particular situation.	○	○	○	○
4 use "雖然······，可是······" to highlight something that is not expected under the given circumstances.	○	○	○	○
5 explain the cultural practice of ushering in good luck and fortune by pasting Lunar New Year couplets on the wall or door.	○	○	○	○
6 write 願意, 參觀, 校園, and 吉利.	○	○	○	○

中國新年
Lunar New Year

My Goals

1 Talk about Lunar New Year customs and their origins
2 Get to know Chinese greetings of luck and fortune
3 Use reduplication of adjectives
4 State the similarity between two concepts
5 Become familiar with Lunar New Year greetings and vocabulary associated with items deemed to be auspicious

1 What does the Chinese word on the wall signify?
2 What are these people doing?

A Based on the pictures, complete the following sentences using the helping phrases.

> **SCENARIO:** Upon meeting each other, 以晴 reminds 久美子 to go to her house during the Lunar New Year.

久美子：聽以安說，這個星期天是中國人的大日子，你們家現在很忙吧？

以　晴：是啊！我們會有很多慶祝活動，

_____

久美子：你們會有慶祝活動，我可以一起參加嗎？

以　晴：我就是要告訴你，這個星期六晚上別忘了來我家吃飯。

久美子：你和我說過嗎？我忘記了。

以　晴：有啊！_____

久美子：我都忘了，安地、阿明都會去嗎？

以　晴：當然，_____

A. 上次我們吃飯的時候，我不是跟妳說過了嗎？

B. 家人、朋友一起來，這樣，吃飯才好玩。

C. 雖然大家都很忙，可是很開心。

D. 讓我們一起做中國菜吧！

B Model on the above text to create a dialogue on inviting a friend to your house for a meal. Your dialogue should incorporate at least two of the sentence structures (highlighted in red) from the above helping phrases.

Vocabulary Builder

gōng xǐ fā cái
恭喜發財

wàn shì rú yì
萬事如意
(may all of your wishes
come true)

gōng hè xīn xǐ
恭賀新禧
(wishing you a happy
New Year)

xīn xiǎng shì chéng
心想事成
(may all of your desires
be fulfilled)

yú
年年有餘
(may there be surpluses
every year)

bù bù gāo shēng
步步高升
(may you rise with
every step)

suì suì píng ān
歲歲平安
(may you be safe through
the years)

jí xiáng rú yì
吉祥如意
(may you have good
fortune in all your affairs)

zhāo cái jìn bǎo
招財進寶
(may you bring in wealth
and fortune)

cái yuán gǔn gǔn
財源滾滾
(may fortune come
rolling in)

kāi zhāng dà jí
開張大吉
(may there be prosperity to
your new beginning)

大吉大利

生日快樂

cháng mìng bǎi suì
長命百歲
(wishing you longevity)

jīn bǎng tí míng
金榜題名
(may you do well in
examinations)

yì fán fēng shùn
一帆風順
(may everything go
smoothly for you)

nián gāo
年糕

fā gāo
發糕
(steamed sponge cake)

jú zi
橘子
(mandarin orange)

魚

shuǐ jiǎo
水餃

chūn lián
春聯
(Lunar New Year
couplets)

biān pào
鞭炮
(firecrackers)

hóng bāo
紅包

New Words

gōng xǐ **恭喜**	congratulations	fā cái **發財**	prosper
yú **餘**	excess	píng ān **平安**	safe
nián gāo **年糕**	glutinous rice cake	shuǐ jiǎo **水餃**	dumpling
hóng bāo **紅包**	red packet		

Mirror Image

1 Split into two teams and stand in two lines facing the board. The last student in each line holds a similarly-sized mirror.

2 The teacher stands behind the two lines and holds up a placard.

3 The student at the end of each line hold up the mirror to decipher the words on the placard through the reflection.

4 He or she will then to write the words or the *pinyin* on the board. The faster one to do so wins a point for the team.

5 If there is an error in writing the word, the next student in turn can amend it.

SCENARIO: Today is the eve of the Lunar New Year. 以晴 has invited her good friends over to her house for the reunion dinner.

明天是中國新年，以晴請她的好朋友來吃年夜飯。

久美子看到門上的「春」和「福」，就說：「我知道這兩個字！中國新年的時候，大門上面要貼這兩個字，而且要倒過來貼。就是春『倒』（到）了！福『倒』（到）了！」以思說：「所以，你們到了！也要『倒過來』！」安地說：「恭喜發財！紅包拿來！」大家聽了，都笑了。原來，以晴已經教過大家，新年的時候，要說過年的吉利話。

吃飯時，他們看見桌上有一條大魚，以思說：「媽媽說今天不可以把魚吃完，要留著明天吃，這樣，以後才會有魚吃，才會『天天有餘』、『年年有餘』。」安地看見水餃時，就說：「我

知道，水餃的樣子很像中國以前的錢，我們把
『錢』吃下去，就會長大一歲。」久美子最喜歡
吃年糕，年糕甜甜的，很好吃。媽媽說，中國字
「高」和「糕」聲音一樣，吃年糕是希望大家一
年比一年高。阿明聽了，又吃了兩塊年糕。

吃完年夜飯，爸爸
拿紅包給大家，說：「這
是中國的壓歲錢，希望大
家在新的一年，❶健健康
康、快快樂樂！」大家都
說中國新年真有趣，吃了
「錢」，可以長大一歲；
吃了年糕可以長高；說了恭喜，就可以發財、
拿紅包。他們希望年年都可以來以晴家過中國新
年。

New Words

xīn nián 新年	New Year	**nián yè fàn** 年夜飯	reunion dinner	**guò nián** 過年	celebrate the New Year
jí lì huà 吉利話	greetings of luck and fortune	**liú** 留	stay	**tián** 甜	sweet
shēng yīn 聲音	sound	**kuài** 塊	(a measure word used for items in pieces or slices)	**yā suì qián** 壓歲錢	money given to children during the Lunar New Year

Exercises

True or False?

Answer the questions according to the reading passage.

對　錯

1. 中國新年那一天，中國人會吃年夜飯。　○　○

2. 怕新年沒有菜吃，所以年夜飯不可以把魚吃完。　○　○

3. 過年吃年糕是因為「糕」的聲音吉利，吃水餃是因為水餃的樣子吉利。　○　○

4. 阿明希望自己再長高一點。　○　○

5. 過年的時候，吃了壓歲錢，就可以長大一歲。　○　○

Think & Discuss

Work in pairs and answer the questions in Chinese.

1. 以晴家吃年夜飯的時候吃了哪些東西？為什麼要吃這些東西？

2. 過年的時候為什麼要把「春」跟「福」倒過來貼？在你住的國家會怎麼慶祝新年？

Culture Link

Why do the Chinese eat dumplings during the Lunar New Year?

The northern Chinese have a tradition of eating dumplings (水餃) during the reunion dinner because it symbolizes an exchange (交) of the old for the new. Furthermore, the dumpling is shaped to resemble the golden ingot used in the past. Eating it is thus believed to bring one fortune and prosperity over the New Year. When preparing it, some people even hide a coin in some dumplings so the people who eat those dumplings would have greater fortune and luck.

The practice of eating dumplings started about 1900 years ago. A physician named Zhang Zhong Jing (張仲景) noticed frostbite on the ears of the poor. To help them to get better, he gathered some herbs which could keep people warm, and stuffed them with mutton and pepper into a pocket of dough shaped like an ear before cooking it. When the poor ate the dumplings, their bodies and ears warmed up and this tradition has been followed ever since.

Beside dumplings, Chinese usually prepare the following items for celebrating Lunar New Year, in the hope that they bring prosperity and safety in the coming new year.

TALK ABOUT IT

The Chinese eat dumplings during the Lunar New Year. Is there a tradition of eating certain food during the New Year or other festivals in your country?

1 | 健健康康
安安靜靜

As an adjective → AABB的

健康 → 媽媽希望孩子健健康康的。

安靜 → 教室裡安安靜靜的。

TIP Previously we learned about the reduplication of single-character adjectives (AA 的 / AA 地). We can also reduplicate adjectives that are made up of two characters (AABB). When adjectives are reduplicated, the description is already intensified and made more vivid. Hence, no further modifiers such as intensifiers (很, 非常) or negative markers (不) may be added.

As an adverbial → AABB地 + Verb

健康 → 媽媽希望孩子健健康康地長大。

安靜 → 學生都安安靜靜地寫功課。

PRACTICE IT Fill in the blanks by reduplicating a suitable adjective from word bank.

1. 我的房間有＿＿＿＿＿＿＿＿＿＿櫃子。

2. 我希望大家＿＿＿＿＿＿＿＿＿＿。

3. 晚上院子裡＿＿＿＿＿＿＿＿＿＿。

4. 小狗＿＿＿＿＿＿＿＿＿＿跑到門前。

5. 學生都＿＿＿＿＿＿＿＿＿去學校上課。

6. 大家在圖書館裡＿＿＿＿＿＿＿＿＿看書。

| 快 |
| 高 |
| 安靜 |
| 快樂 |
| 健康 |

Go500 WANT TO LEARN MORE?

Check out the Text > Sentence Pattern section on the Go500 CD.

Listening

Go 500

Text > Dialogue section

SCENARIO: 以晴 is having her reunion dinner with her family and good friends. This is the first time her friends are celebrating the Lunar New Year and they have many questions to ask Sunny's mother.

 A Listen to the Go 500 CD for the dialogue and answer the following multiple-choice questions.

1. 中國人過年的時候會做什麼？

   (A) 吃麵　(B) 發紅包　(C) 看唱歌比賽

2. 日本新年在哪一天？

   (A) 比美國新年早一天

   (B) 跟中國新年同一天

   (C) 一月一日

3. 為什麼過年可以拿壓歲錢？

   (A) 紅包是紅色的，很吉利。

   (B) 大人希望把小孩的壞運壓下去。

   (C) 小孩過年得壓著紅包睡覺。

4. 要介紹中國新年，下面哪些是對的？

   (A) 在一月一日

   (B) 吃年糕和水餃

   (C) 用唱歌比賽來慶祝

   (D) 發紅包希望小孩平安長大。

   (E) 要多說好話讓大家運氣好。

New Words

發 fā	give
大人 dà rén	adults
壓/壓著 yā / yā zhe	pressed down; suppress

中國新年　　123

( )　安　　地：Cindy 阿姨，為什麼新年拿的紅包叫壓歲錢？

　　媽　　媽：因為拿到紅包以後，晚上睡覺的時候，要壓著紅包睡，把過去一年的＿＿＿＿＿都「壓下去」，＿＿＿＿＿＿才可以平安長大。

( )　久美子：這是我第一次到中國人的家裡吃年夜飯，真有趣。

　　以　　晴：日本新年是哪一天？也吃水餃和年糕嗎？

　　久美子：❷日本新年跟美國新年一樣，都是＿＿＿＿＿＿＿＿＿。在日本過新年的時候，我們吃麵、吃年糕，也拿＿＿＿＿＿＿，還有＿＿＿＿＿＿＿，大家一起來慶祝新年。

( )　久美子：我今天學了很多中文，而且，都是吉利話。我希望大家春到，福到，恭喜發財，大吉大利！

　　以　　晴：還有長一點的吉利話：恭喜恭喜＿＿＿＿＿＿，好運來，壞運走，＿＿＿＿＿＿＿＿＿＿！

( )　以　　思：媽媽，什麼是吉利話？

　　媽　　媽：吉利話就是＿＿＿＿＿＿。「大吉大利」就是「運氣好，多發財」的意思。過年的時候，要多說吉利話，讓大家＿＿＿＿＿＿＿。

　　安　　地：美國也有新年，可是不像中國和日本的新年那麼＿＿＿＿＿＿，有好吃的東西，還可以拿壓歲錢。

C   Listen to the conversation on the Go500 CD again, and fill in the blanks.

Language Focus

日本新年 (xīn nián)	跟	美國新年 (xīn nián)	一樣，都	是一月一日。
恭喜發財 (gōng xǐ fā cái)		年年有餘 (yú)		是吉利話。(jí lì huà)

②

A: 中國人過年的時候，常常吃水餃嗎？ (guò nián) (shuǐ jiǎo)

B: 水餃跟年糕一樣，都是中國人 (shuǐ jiǎo) (nián gāo)
過年要吃的東西。 (guò nián)

A: 你們班上的新同學從哪一國來？

B: 他跟安地一樣，都是英國人。

> **TIP** This construction links two similar concepts and spells out the similarity at the end of the sentence. The two phrases joined by 跟 are usually of the same word class and they typically share a basis for comparison.

 **PRACTICE IT**

Using sentence structure 2, complete the dialogues with the helping phrases.

1. A: 你吃過皮蛋嗎？

   B: _____

2. A: 中國菜容易做嗎？

   B: _____

3. A: 以安、以思也要做家事嗎？

   B: _____

┌ Group A ┐	→ ┌ Group B
日本菜	好吃，不容易做
以晴	要做家事
安地	不敢吃皮蛋

Culture Link

Of the many stories explaining the origins of 壓歲錢, one of them tells of how 壓歲錢 was meant to calm one's nerves (壓驚 yā jīng). Legend has it that a ferocious man-eating creature named 年 would appear every 365 days to harm people. The adults would light firecrackers to frighten the monster away and use food to calm the children's nerves. Gradually, food was substituted by money and this tradition has been followed since 1000 years ago.

In China, children receive 壓歲錢 during the Lunar New Year. Is there a similar practice or tradition in your country?

Role Playing

Form groups of five and role-play the scenario. You may use the sentence structures provided below.

CHARACTERS:

孫媽媽, 以晴, 以思, 安地, 久美子

SCENARIO:
After the reunion dinner, Sunny's mother is going to distribute 壓歲錢. However, the children have to say a greeting for good fortune and state their wishes for the New Year before receiving their 壓歲錢.

SENTENCE STRUCTURES:

1. 希望……

2. AABB（Reduplication of adjectives）

3. ……跟……一樣，都……

4. ……，這樣，……才……

5. 怎麼可以……呢？

Learn about the Chinese Language & Culture

過年的時候中國人會在紅紙上寫兩個句子，再貼在大門的兩邊，這叫做「春聯」，也叫「＊對聯」。中國人＊相信大門上貼上春聯，可以帶來好運。

你想寫春聯嗎？在寫春聯前，你要知道這些事：

第一，兩個句子的字要一樣多。

第二，兩個句子在同一個＊位置的＊詞，＊詞性要一樣。如果第一句的前兩個字是＊名詞，第二句的前兩個字也要是名詞。

第三，第一句的最後一字要用三＊聲、四聲的字；第二句的最後一字要用一聲、二聲的字。＊大部分的春聯你都可以用這個＊方法找出哪個是第一句和第二句。

第四，第一句貼在門的右邊，也叫做上聯。第二句貼在門的左邊，叫做下聯。兩個句子的意思要有關係。

現在中國人不是只有在過年的時候才在門上貼春聯。不是過年的時候，我們也可以在很多＊地方看到春聯。

＊對聯 Spring couplets   相信 believe   位置 position   詞 word   詞性 word class   名詞 noun

……聲 tone   大部分 majority   方法 way; method   地方 place

Work It Out

Be it the food eaten or the celebratory activities, the arrival of the New Year is celebrated in different ways around the world.

TASK

New Year Festivities Around the World

1 Form a small group. Each group chooses a country to work on.

2 Use the Internet to find out about the following aspects:
- Duration of the celebration
- Food eaten and its significance
- Dressing and traditional costumes
- Special rituals
- Special celebratory activities

3 The teacher lists these countries on the board. In turns, each group contributes information in a sentence on the country they research on.

LEARNING LOG

I can...

		Excellent	Good	Fair	Need Improvement
1	state the origins of traditions observed during the Lunar New Year.	○	○	○	○
2	use greetings of luck and fortune to wish people well.	○	○	○	○
3	use reduplication of adjectives in the form of AABB in sentences.	○	○	○	○
4	use the sentence structure "……跟……一樣，都……" to describe the similarity between two concepts.	○	○	○	○
5	write 恭喜, 發財, 壓歲錢, and 平安.	○	○	○	○

有趣的中國字

Interesting Chinese Characters

My Goals

1 Can you guess all the words shown above?

2 What do they have in common?

1 Understand the meaning of a character by identifying its components

2 Convey the sudden realization of a fact

3 Express my personal opinion or offer a suggestion

4 Recognize the different positions and written forms of radicals

5 Become familiar with common radicals

Get Started

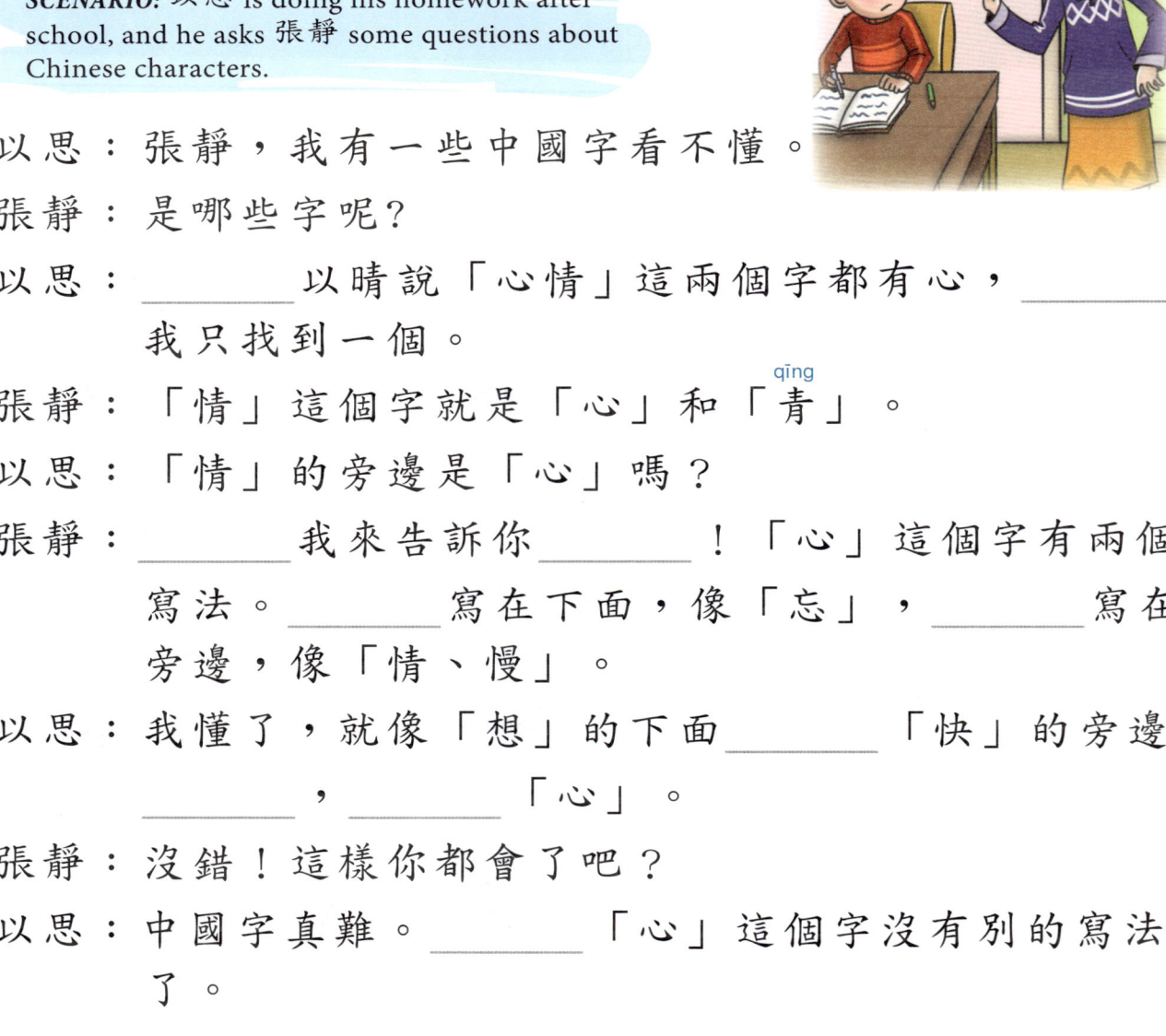

A Complete the following dialogue with the sentence structures provided.

SCENARIO: 以思 is doing his homework after school, and he asks 張靜 some questions about Chinese characters.

以思：張靜，我有一些中國字看不懂。

張靜：是哪些字呢？

以思：_____以晴說「心情」這兩個字都有心，_____ 我只找到一個。

張靜：「情」這個字就是「心」和「青」。

以思：「情」的旁邊是「心」嗎？

張靜：_____我來告訴你_____！「心」這個字有兩個寫法。_____寫在下面，像「忘」，_____寫在旁邊，像「情、慢」。

以思：我懂了，就像「想」的下面_____「快」的旁邊 _____，_____「心」。

張靜：沒錯！這樣你都會了吧？

以思：中國字真難。_____「心」這個字沒有別的寫法了。

A. 讓……吧	B. 希望……
C. 有的……，有的……	D. 雖然……，可是……
E. ……跟……一樣，都是……	

B In pairs, take on the roles of the two characters above and read aloud the completed dialogue. Exchange roles and repeat the exercise.

Vocabulary Builder

心 ▶ 思、情

手 ▶ 打

水 ▶ 清

火 ▶ 燒、熱

cǎo 艸 ▶ 花

zhú 竹 ▶ 筆

yán 言 ▶ 說

mù 木 ▶ 櫃

目 ▶ 眼

mì 糸 ▶ 紅

shí 食 ▶ 飯

yǎn 广 ▶ 店

chuáng 疒 ▶ 病

mián 宀 ▶ 家

chuò 辵 ▶ 過

---

cōng míng 聰明 ◀▶ bèn 笨 (stupid)

qīng chǔ 清楚 ◀▶ mó hú 模糊 (confused)

zhèng cháng 正常 (normal) ◀▶ qí guài 奇怪

ān xīn 安心 ◀▶ fán nǎo 煩惱 (troubled)

Ready, Construction, Action!

聰明
不聰明
聰不聰明？
聰明不聰明？

1 The teacher explains the constructions on the right and discusses with the students to determine actions representing the various constructions.

2 Each student prepares four slips of paper. Choose a word from the list on the left and model on the constructions on the right. Write each construction on a slip of paper. Then, drop the four slips of paper into a box.

3 The teacher randomly picks a slip of paper from the box and recites the construction on it. Students have to act out the construction.

4 Those who make mistakes have to go to the front to pick a slip and recite the construction. The last student left wins the game.

New Words

cōng míng	qīng chǔ	qí guài	ān xīn
聰明 | intelligent	清楚 | clear; lucid	奇怪 | strange	安心 | be at ease

SCENARIO: Both 以思 and 以安 are learning Chinese. One day, they talk about their Chinese names.

　　有一天，以思在練習寫自己的中文名字。他笑著對以安說：「以安！你知道嗎？你的中文名字裡有個『女』生的『女』，❶孫以安原來是一個女生啊！」以安對弟弟說：「你的中文名字才
<ruby>奇<rt>qí</rt></ruby><ruby>怪<rt>guài</rt></ruby>呢！有這麼多<ruby>方<rt>fāng</rt></ruby><ruby>塊<rt>kuài</rt></ruby>壓在『心』的上面，所以才學不好中文。」

　　媽媽聽見他們<ruby>吵<rt>chǎo</rt></ruby>來<ruby>吵<rt>chǎo</rt></ruby>去，就說：「不要<ruby>吵<rt>chǎo</rt></ruby>，你們的中文名字是媽媽取的，都很有意思，我來說給你們聽。『安』這個字，原來是說一個家，有了<ruby>女<rt>nǚ</rt></ruby><ruby>人<rt>rén</rt></ruby>，就能讓人<ruby>安<rt>ān</rt></ruby><ruby>心<rt>xīn</rt></ruby>。媽媽覺得以安能讓我<ruby>安<rt>ān</rt></ruby><ruby>心<rt>xīn</rt></ruby>，所以，給以安取了這個名字。」

　　媽媽又對以思說：「你知道你為什麼叫以思嗎？『思』的上面是<ruby>腦<rt>nǎo</rt></ruby>，下面有『心』，媽媽希望以思用<ruby>腦<rt>nǎo</rt></ruby>又用心，不要忘了這個，忘了那個。『忘』這個字，就是心『死』了。」以安笑著說：「對啊！❷我覺得以思的名字<ruby>應<rt>yīng</rt></ruby><ruby>該<rt>gāi</rt></ruby>叫『孫以忘』最好！」

以晴問媽媽：「為什麼『思』的心在下面，『情』的『心』卻在左邊？」媽媽說：「你看，『情』這個字，左邊的字和右邊的字，都是長長的，是不是站_{zhàn}起來才好看？『思』這個字，上面的字和下面的字，都是方方的，是不是坐下來才好看？」

以晴笑著說：「啊！我知道了！所以，以安和以思才會喜歡天天『坐』著打電腦，以晴才會喜歡天天跑出去『站_{zhàn}』著玩。」

New Words

fāng kuài 方塊 | block; cube	chǎo 吵 | argue; quarrel	nǚ rén 女人 | woman	nǎo 腦 | brain
yīng gāi 應該 | should	zhàn 站 | stand		

Culture Link

Radicals in Chinese Characters

Some radicals can stand alone as independent characters and they can also combine with other components to form other characters. Some of these radicals may appear in the same form in all instances, while others are written in different forms, such as 人、心、手, and 水.

Such radicals may be written in a different form or position when combined with different components so that the characters look more pleasing or proportionate. For example, the radical 人 may be written as 亻(as in 你 and 他), 心 may be written as 忄(as in 情 and 快), 手 may be written as 扌(as in 打), and 水 may be written as 氵(as in 洗 and 清).

Exercises

Answer the questions according to the passage.

對　錯

1. 媽媽覺得以安跟女人一樣，讓她安心。　　○　○
<small>nǚ rén</small>　　<small>ān xīn</small>

2. 媽媽覺得以思常常不用心，所以給他取名字叫
以思。　　○　○

3. 「亡」的意思就是「死」。　　○　○
<small>wáng</small>

4. 「心」放在字的左邊或下面，意思都一樣。　　○　○

5. 以晴喜歡在外面玩，以安、以思喜歡留在家裡。　　○　○

Think & Discuss

Work in pairs and answer the questions in Chinese.

1. 以晴的媽媽為什麼給兩個兒子取名字叫「以安」和
「以思」？

2. 以晴的媽媽怎麼介紹「忘」這個字？試試看，用自己
的想法介紹一個字。

Group the following characters according to their radicals.

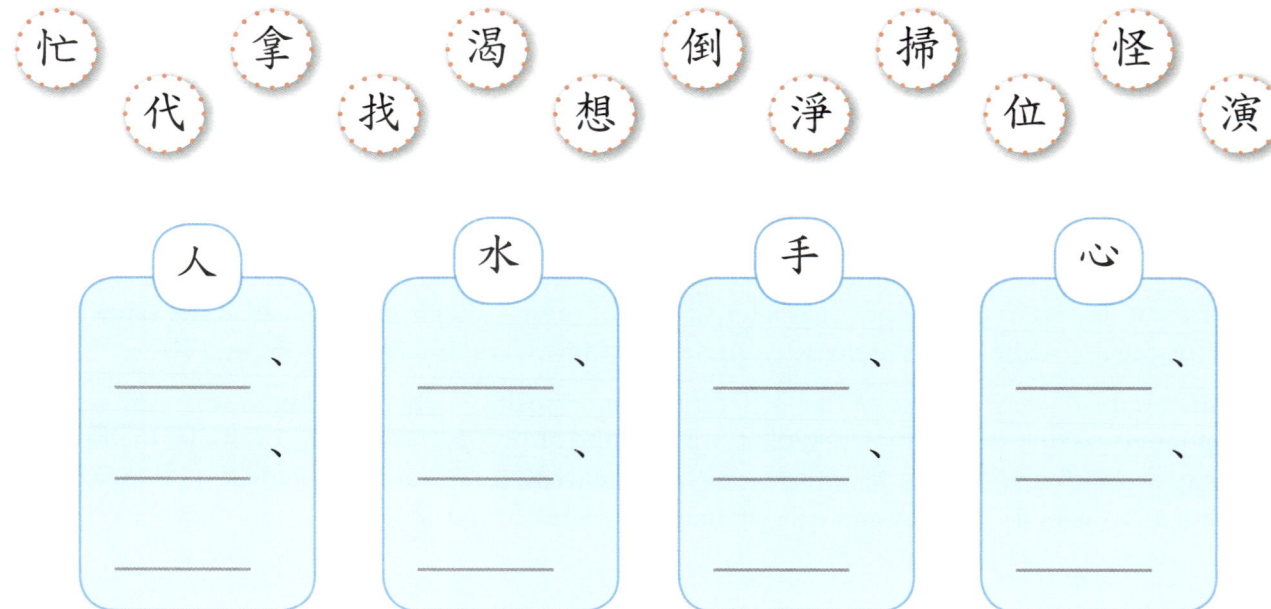

忙　拿　渴　倒　掃　怪
代　找　想　淨　位　演

人	水	手	心
、	、	、	、
、	、	、	、

Language Focus

孫以安	原來	是一個女生	啊！
壓歲錢		就是紅包	

1

A: 下午我要去安地家跟他一起練習中文。

B: 安地原來會說中文啊！

A: 這個星期天我要去白爺爺家。

B: 原來你也認識白爺爺啊！

TIP This sentence structure suggests that the speaker has a sudden realization of a fact that he did not know previously. 原來 may be positioned before or after the subject. Thus, the first example can also be rephrased as "原來孫以安是一個女生啊！"

PRACTICE IT

Based on the scenarios, make sentences using sentence structure 1 and the helping phrase.

1. 雖然以晴的爸爸是美國人，可是他卻會說中文。你對以晴說……

_____

2. 你跟同學買了一樣的小說。你對同學說……

_____

3. 你在客廳的椅子下面，找到自己的棒球帽。你說……

_____

在這裡　　喜歡這本小說　　學過中文

2	我覺得	以思的名字應該叫「孫以忘」	最好！
		yīng gāi	
		過年的時候回家吃年夜飯	

A: 我們應該怎麼取中文名字
最好？
（yīng gāi）

B: 我覺得懂中文的朋友幫
我們取中文名字最好！

A: 過年的時候我們要吃什麼？

B: 我覺得過年的時候吃水餃
最好！

TIP This sentence structure conveys the speaker's personal opinion or suggestion. The tone used must not be too harsh or the speaker may be perceived as being too forceful in his opinion or suggestion. It is best to refrain from using this sentence structure with one's elders and superiors, or with people he has just met.

PRACTICE IT

Using sentence structure 2, complete the dialogues with the helping phrases.

1. A: 你們中午想做什麼菜？

   B: _____

2. A: 明天我們怎麼去學校？

   B: _____

3. A: 我們應該去哪裡看書？
   （yīng gāi）

   B: _____

| 走路 |
| 麻婆豆腐 |
| 圖書館 |

Check out the Text > Sentence Pattern section on the Go500 CD.

 Listening

Go 500

Text > Dialogue section

SCENARIO: Mother and 以晴 are in the kitchen having a discussion on the meanings behind their Chinese names.

A Listen to the Go500 CD for the dialogue and answer the following multiple-choice questions.

1. 下面哪一個不是「青」的意思？
   (A) 水 (B) 美 (C) 好

2. 媽媽為什麼覺得以晴聰明？
   (A)「晴」就是聰明的意思。
   (B) 以晴知道「靜」跟「晴」一樣，都有「青」。
   (C) 媽媽說了「青」的意思，以晴就懂了。

3. 以思覺得以安跟誰在一起不會爭吵？
   (A) 以晴 (B) 張靜 (C) 久美子

4. 為什麼以思覺得以晴可憐？
   (A) 媽媽不愛以晴。
   (B) 以晴的名字跟媽媽的名字沒關係。
   (C) 只有以晴是女生。

5. 寫出下面這三個字的意思：
   (A) 請：＿＿＿＿＿＿＿＿
   (B) 晴：＿＿＿＿＿＿＿＿
   (C) 清：＿＿＿＿＿＿＿＿

New Words

zhēng chǎo 爭吵	quarrel
fā xiàn 發現	discover
qīng qīng sè 青／青色	green
kě lián 可憐	pitiful

有趣的中國字　　137

以思：所以，以安和張靜在一起，就很安靜不會爭吵（zhēng chǎo），對不對？媽媽！

以安：媽媽我覺得妳知道很多東西，也＿＿＿＿＿＿＿＿＿＿。妳的中文名字是「心如」，我中文名字的「安」，裡面有妳名字的「＿＿＿」，弟弟中文名字的「思」，裡面也有妳中文名字的「＿＿＿」。

以晴：我知道了，就好像是「請」是＿＿＿＿＿＿＿，所以要常常說「請」。「清」就是＿＿＿＿＿＿＿＿＿＿很「清」，看要看清楚（qīng chǔ），說要說清（qīng）楚（chǔ），聽也要聽清楚。

媽媽：以晴好聰明（cōng míng），媽媽一說妳＿＿＿＿＿＿＿＿＿＿。

以思：我知道媽媽最愛＿＿＿＿＿＿＿＿＿，因為，哥哥有媽媽的「女」，我有媽媽的「心」，可是，可憐（kě lián）的以晴，什麼都沒有。

媽媽：誰說的？以晴姓孫，是＿＿＿＿＿＿＿＿，英文名字叫Sunny 也有媽媽的姓，媽媽覺得以晴是孫家的「＿＿＿＿＿」，你們說，媽媽愛不愛以晴呢？

以晴：媽媽！我發現張靜和我的名字都有「青」
這個字，只是我的「青」在右邊，她的「青」
在左邊。

媽媽：「青」是青色，也是「美」和「好」的意
思。妳的「晴」是＿＿＿＿＿＿＿＿＿。
張靜的「靜」，左邊是「好」，右邊是爭
吵的「爭」，就是「安靜」、「不爭吵」
的意思。

C Listen to the conversation on the Go500 CD again, and fill in the blanks.

Role Playing

Form groups of four and role-play the scenario. You may use the sentence structures provided below.

CHARACTERS:

以晴，以安，以思，安地

SCENARIO:

安地 is studying at Sunny's (以晴) house. He has some difficulty with some Chinese words and 以思 volunteers to help him. However, 以晴 and 以安 do not feel that 以思 is proficient enough to help 安地. 以思 is indignant about their reaction and so 以晴 and 以安 decide to test him.

SENTENCE STRUCTURES:

1. 原來……啊！
2. 我覺得……最好！
3. 希望……
4. ……跟……一樣，都……

在Go500我們學到四種中文 *造字的 *方法：人們看著天上的太陽、月亮寫出「日」、「月」，是 *象形；在一條 *線加上 *記號，*表示「上」、「下」，是 *指事；用聲音來表示更多的字，像是「枝」，是 *形聲；手放眼睛 *上方表示「看」，是 *會意；每個中文字都有一個故事。

現在你學新的中文字的時候，也能說說這個字的故事，讓學中文字更有趣。

*造字 character construction　　方法 method　　月亮 moon　　象形 pictograph　　線 line　　加上 add

記號 mark　　表示 symbolize　　指事 explanatory　　形聲 picto-phonetic　　上方 on top of ; above

會意 characters made up of associative components

Try It Out

A Can you identify the Chinese character and its construction method in each of the following picture? Write the Chinese characters in the squares, and their character construction methods in the circles.

ⓐ 象形　　ⓑ 指事　　ⓒ 會意　　ⓓ 形聲

1.

2.

3.

4.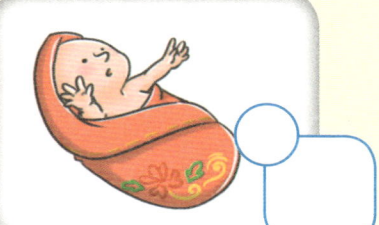

B Using the pictures as clues, explain how these scenarios led to the formation of the six characters.

Work It Out

Chinese characters are indeed interesting. From all the Chinese words you have learned, which ones do you think are the most interesting? Write them down and discuss them with your classmates.

TASK

Word Spar

1 Write down eight words you find interesting in the first row of the table below.

2 In turns, read out the words on your list to the class, one word per turn.

3 Conduct a tally at the same time and fill in the second row of the table.

4 Record the word with the highest score from the tally and write down why you find this word interesting.

5 Look for two other classmates who find the same word interesting, and write down their reasons in the table.

Eight words I find interesting:								
Number of classmates who find these words interesting as well:								
The word with the highest score from the tally is:								
I find this word interesting because:								
(classmate's name) finds this _____ word interesting because:								
(classmate's name) finds this _____ word interesting because:								

LEARNING LOG

I can...

		Excellent	Good	Fair	Need Improvement
1	explain Chinese characters by breaking them down into their components.	○	○	○	○
2	use "……原來……啊！" to convey a sudden realization of a fact.	○	○	○	○
3	use "我覺得……最好！" to express my personal opinion or to offer a suggestion.	○	○	○	○
4	recognize the different written forms of the radicals 人, 水, 手, and 心.	○	○	○	○
5	write 聰明, 應該, 清楚, and 爭吵.	○	○	○	○

Vocabulary Index

Words marked with an asterisk (*) are supplementary vocabulary from each lesson. They are included to supplement students' vocabulary and enhance their oral proficiency.

Pinyin	Bopomofo	Traditional Character	English	Simplified Character	Lesson
A					
a	˙ㄚ	啊	ah (an exclamation)		L5
ā	ㄚ	阿	(a prefix attached to names, surnames, or kinship terms to form terms of endearment, e.g. 阿明, 阿爸.)		L2
ā yí	ㄚ ㄧˊ	阿姨	aunty		L5
āi jí	ㄞ ㄐㄧˊ	埃及*	Egypt		L2
ài qíng	ㄞˋ ㄑㄧㄥˊ	愛情*	romance	爱情	L4
ān xīn	ㄢ ㄒㄧㄣ	安心	be at ease		L10
ào dà lì yà	ㄠˋ ㄉㄚˋ ㄌㄧˋ ㄧㄚˋ	澳大利亞*	Australia	澳大利亚	L2
B					
ba	˙ㄅㄚ	吧	(exclamation tag)		L7
bā xī	ㄅㄚ ㄒㄧ	巴西*	Brazil		L2
bāng zhù	ㄅㄤ ㄓㄨˋ	幫助*	help	帮助	L8
bàng	ㄅㄤˋ	棒	excellent		L4
bèi dòng	ㄅㄟˋ ㄉㄨㄥˋ	被動*	passive	被动	L3
bèn	ㄅㄣˋ	笨*	stupid		L10
biān pào	ㄅㄧㄢ ㄆㄠˋ	鞭炮*	firecrackers		L9
biàn	ㄅㄧㄢˋ	變	change	变	L6
bīng xiāng	ㄅㄧㄥ ㄒㄧㄤ	冰箱*	refrigerator		L7
bù bù gāo shēng	ㄅㄨˋ ㄅㄨˋ ㄍㄠ ㄕㄥ	步步高升*	may you rise with every step		L9
bú guò	ㄅㄨˊ ㄍㄨㄛˋ	不過	but; however	不过	L2
bú xiàng	ㄅㄨˊ ㄒㄧㄤˋ	不像*	different		L1
C					
cā chuāng hù	ㄘㄚ ㄔㄨㄤ ㄏㄨˋ	擦窗戶*	wipe the windows	擦窗户	L6
cā gān wǎn pán	ㄘㄚ ㄍㄢ ㄨㄢˇ ㄆㄢˊ	擦乾碗盤*	dry the dishes	擦干碗盘	L6
cā liú lǐ tái	ㄘㄚ ㄌㄧㄡˊ ㄌㄧˇ ㄊㄞˊ	擦流理台*	wipe the kitchen counter	擦流理台	L6

cái yuán gǔn gǔn	ㄘㄞˊ ㄩㄢˊ ㄍㄨㄣˇ ㄍㄨㄣˇ	財源滾滾*	may fortune come rolling in	财源滚滚	L9
cài dāo	ㄘㄞˋ ㄉㄠ	菜刀*	knife	菜刀	L7
cān guān	ㄘㄢ ㄍㄨㄢ	參觀	visit	参观	L8
cān guǎn	ㄘㄢ ㄍㄨㄢˇ	餐館	restaurant	餐馆	L3
cǎo	ㄘㄠˇ	艸*	(a Chinese radical meaning grass)	艹	L10
cōng	ㄘㄨㄥ	蔥*	green onion	葱	L5
cōng míng	ㄘㄨㄥ ㄇㄧㄥˊ	聰明	smart	聪明	L1*/L10
cù	ㄘㄨˋ	醋*	vinegar		L5
cháng mìng bǎi suì	ㄔㄤˊ ㄇㄧㄥˋ ㄅㄞˇ ㄙㄨㄟˋ	長命百歲*	wishing you longevity	长命百岁	L9
chǎo	ㄔㄠˇ	炒*	stir-fry		L7
chǎo	ㄔㄠˇ	吵	argue; quarrel		L10
chéng gōng	ㄔㄥˊ ㄍㄨㄥ	成功*	successful		L1
chéng shí	ㄔㄥˊ ㄕˊ	誠實*	honest	诚实	L3
chū bǎn shè	ㄔㄨ ㄅㄢˇ ㄕㄜˋ	出版社*	publisher		L4
chū shēng	ㄔㄨ ㄕㄥ	出生	born		L2
chū zhōng	ㄔㄨ ㄓㄨㄥ	初中	junior high school		L2
chù diàn	ㄔㄨˋ ㄉㄧㄢˋ	觸電	electric shock	触电	L7
chuáng	ㄔㄨㄤˊ	疒*	(a Chinese radical meaning illness)		L10
chūn lián	ㄔㄨㄣ ㄌㄧㄢˊ	春聯*	Lunar New Year couplets	春联	L9
chuò	ㄔㄨㄛˋ	辵*	(a Chinese radical meaning walking)	辶	L10

D

dà fāng	ㄉㄚˋ ㄈㄤ	大方*	generous		L3
dà jí dà lì	ㄉㄚˋ ㄐㄧˊ ㄉㄚˋ ㄌㄧˋ	大吉大利	good luck and good fortune		L8
dà mén	ㄉㄚˋ ㄇㄣˊ	大門	gate; main entrance	大门	L8
dà rén	ㄉㄚˋ ㄖㄣˊ	大人	adults		L9
dà suàn	ㄉㄚˋ ㄙㄨㄢˋ	大蒜*	garlic	大蒜	L5
dàn	ㄉㄢˋ	蛋	egg		L5
dàn huā tāng	ㄉㄢˋ ㄏㄨㄚ ㄊㄤ	蛋花湯*	egg drop soup	蛋花汤	L5
dàn shì	ㄉㄢˋ ㄕˋ	但是	but; however		L6
dāng rán	ㄉㄤ ㄖㄢˊ	當然	definitely	当然	L6

dào / dào guò lái	ㄉㄠˋ/ㄉㄠˋ ㄍㄨㄛˋ ㄌㄞˊ	倒/倒過來	upside down	倒/倒过来	L8
dào lè sè	ㄉㄠˋ ㄌㄜˋ ㄙㄜˋ	倒垃圾*	dispose of the rubbish		L6
dào (shuǐ)	ㄉㄠˋ （ㄕㄨㄟˇ）	倒(水)*	pour (water)		L7
dé guó	ㄉㄜˊ ㄍㄨㄛˊ	德國*	Germany	德国	L2
diàn guō	ㄉㄧㄢˋ ㄍㄨㄛ	電鍋	rice cooker	电锅	L7
dǒng	ㄉㄨㄥˇ	懂	understand	懂	L2
dòu fu	ㄉㄡˋ ˙ㄈㄨ	豆腐	tofu; bean curd		L5
dòu zi	ㄉㄡˋ ˙ㄗ	豆子*	beans		L5
dú lì	ㄉㄨˊ ㄌㄧˋ	獨立*	independent	独立	L3
dú shū	ㄉㄨˊ ㄕㄨ	讀書	study	读书	L2
dùn	ㄉㄨㄣˋ	燉	stew	炖	L7

E

ér qiě	ㄦˊ ㄑㄧㄝˇ	而且	furthermore		L4

F

fā	ㄈㄚ	發	give	发	L9
fā cái	ㄈㄚ ㄘㄞˊ	發財	prosper	发财	L9
fā gāo	ㄈㄚ ㄍㄠ	發糕*	steamed sponge cake	发糕	L9
fā xiàn	ㄈㄚ ㄒㄧㄢˋ	發現	discover	发现	L10
fǎ guó	ㄈㄚˇ ㄍㄨㄛˊ	法國*	France	法国	L2
fān yì	ㄈㄢ ㄧˋ	翻譯*	translator	翻译	L4
fán nǎo	ㄈㄢˊ ㄋㄠˇ	煩惱*	troubled	烦恼	L10
fāng kuài	ㄈㄤ ㄎㄨㄞˋ	方塊	block; cube	方块	L10
fù guì	ㄈㄨˋ ㄍㄨㄟˋ	富貴*	rich and influential	富贵	L1
fù zé	ㄈㄨˋ ㄗㄜˊ	負責*	responsible	负责	L3

G

gǎn	ㄍㄢˇ	敢	dare		L5
gè xìng	ㄍㄜˋ ㄒㄧㄥˋ	個性*	personality	个性	L3
gēn	ㄍㄣ	跟	with		L3
gōng hè xīn xǐ	ㄍㄨㄥ ㄏㄜˋ ㄒㄧㄣ ㄒㄧˇ	恭賀新禧*	wishing you a happy New Year	恭贺新禧	L9
gōng xǐ	ㄍㄨㄥ ㄒㄧˇ	恭喜	congratulations		L9
gù shì	ㄍㄨˋ ㄕˋ	故事	story		L4
gù shì shū	ㄍㄨˋ ㄕˋ ㄕㄨ	故事書	story book	故事书	L4

guān huǒ	ㄍㄨㄢ ㄏㄨㄛˇ	關火	turn off the fire (of stove)	关火	L7
guì zi	ㄍㄨㄟˋ ·ㄗ	櫃子	locker	柜子	L8
guō zi	ㄍㄨㄛ ·ㄗ	鍋子*	pot	锅子	L7
guò nián	ㄍㄨㄛˋ ㄋㄧㄢˊ	過年	celebrate the New Year	过年	L9

H

hái zi	ㄏㄞˊ ·ㄗ	孩子*	children		L1
hài xiū	ㄏㄞˋ ㄒㄧㄡ	害羞*	shy	害羞	L3
hǎo xiàng	ㄏㄠˇ ㄒㄧㄤˋ	好像	seem		L4
hào kè	ㄏㄠˋ ㄎㄜˋ	好客*	hospitable		L3
hóng bāo	ㄏㄨㄥˊ ㄅㄠ	紅包	red packet	红包	L9
hú jiāo fěn	ㄏㄨˊ ㄐㄧㄠ ㄈㄣˇ	胡椒粉*	pepper		L5
huā shēng	ㄏㄨㄚ ㄕㄥ	花生	peanut	花生	L1
huá dǎo	ㄏㄨㄚˊ ㄉㄠˇ	滑倒*	slip and fall	滑倒	L7
huá rén	ㄏㄨㄚˊ ㄖㄣˊ	華人	Chinese (people)	华人	L1
huá wén	ㄏㄨㄚˊ ㄨㄣˊ	華文*	Chinese language	华文	L1
huài rén	ㄏㄨㄞˋ ㄖㄣˊ	壞人	villain	坏人	L4
huān yíng	ㄏㄨㄢ ㄧㄥˊ	歡迎	welcome	欢迎	L6
huán jìng	ㄏㄨㄢˊ ㄐㄧㄥˋ	環境*	environment; surroundings	环境	L8
huì zhě	ㄏㄨㄟˋ ㄓㄜˇ	繪者*	illustrator	绘者	L4
huó pō	ㄏㄨㄛˊ ㄆㄛ	活潑*	vivacious	活泼	L3
huǒ	ㄏㄨㄛˇ	火	fire		L7

J

jí	ㄐㄧˊ	吉	lucky; auspicious		L8
jì / jì zhù	ㄐㄧˋ / ㄐㄧˋ ㄓㄨˋ	記/記住	remember	记/记住	L1
jí lì huà	ㄐㄧˊ ㄌㄧˋ ㄏㄨㄚˋ	吉利話	greetings of luck and fortune	吉利话	L9
jí xiáng rú yì	ㄐㄧˊ ㄒㄧㄤˊ ㄖㄨˊ ㄧˋ	吉祥如意*	may you have good fortune in all your affairs		L9
jiā ná dà	ㄐㄧㄚ ㄋㄚˊ ㄉㄚˋ	加拿大*	Canada		L2
jiā rè	ㄐㄧㄚ ㄖㄜˋ	加熱*	heat	加热	L7
jiā rén	ㄐㄧㄚ ㄖㄣˊ	家人	family		L1
jiā shì	ㄐㄧㄚ ㄕˋ	家事	housework; household chores		L6
jiān	ㄐㄧㄢ	煎*	pan fry		L7

jiǎn chá	ㄐㄧㄢˇ ㄔㄚˊ	檢查	check	检查	L7
jiàng yóu	ㄐㄧㄤˋ ㄧㄡˊ	醬油*	soy sauce	酱油	L5
jiāo huā	ㄐㄧㄠ ㄏㄨㄚ	澆花*	water the plants	浇花	L6
jiāo péng yǒu	ㄐㄧㄠ ㄆㄥˊ ㄧㄡˇ	交朋友	make friends		L3
jié	ㄐㄧㄝˊ	節	session	节	L7
jiě mèi	ㄐㄧㄝˇ ㄇㄟˋ	姊妹*	sisters	姐妹	L1
jiè shào	ㄐㄧㄝˋ ㄕㄠˋ	介紹	introduce	介绍	L1
jīn bǎng tí míng	ㄐㄧㄣ ㄅㄤˇ ㄊㄧˊ ㄇㄧㄥˊ	金榜題名*	may you do well in examinations	金榜题名	L9
jiù	ㄐㄧㄡˋ	舊	old	旧	L8
jú zi	ㄐㄩˊ ˙ㄗ	橘子*	mandarin orange		L9
jué de	ㄐㄩㄝˊ ˙ㄉㄜ	覺得	feel; think	觉得	L1

K

kāi huǒ	ㄎㄞ ㄏㄨㄛˇ	開火*	turn on the fire (of stove)	开火	L7
kāi lǎng	ㄎㄞ ㄌㄤˇ	開朗*	cheerful	开朗	L3
kāi zhāng dà jí	ㄎㄞ ㄓㄤ ㄉㄚˋ ㄐㄧˊ	開張大吉*	may there be prosperity to your new beginning	开张大吉	L9
kǎo	ㄎㄠˇ	烤*	roast		L7
kǎo xiāng	ㄎㄠˇ ㄒㄧㄤ	烤箱*	oven		L7
kē pǔ shū	ㄎㄜ ㄆㄨˇ ㄕㄨ	科普書*	popular science book	科普书	L4
kě lián	ㄎㄜˇ ㄌㄧㄢˊ	可憐	pitiful	可怜	L10
kě pà	ㄎㄜˇ ㄆㄚˋ	可怕	frightening		L4
kǒng bù	ㄎㄨㄥˇ ㄅㄨˋ	恐怖*	horror		L4
kū	ㄎㄨ	哭	cry		L1
kǔ	ㄎㄨˇ	苦*	bitter	苦	L5
kuài	ㄎㄨㄞˋ	塊	(a measure word used for items in pieces or slices)	块	L9

L

là	ㄌㄚˋ	辣*	spicy; hot		L5
là jiāo	ㄌㄚˋ ㄐㄧㄠ	辣椒*	chili		L5
lǎo xiān shēng	ㄌㄠˇ ㄒㄧㄢ ㄕㄥ	老先生	old man		L3
lè guān	ㄌㄜˋ ㄍㄨㄢ	樂觀*	optimistic	乐观	L3
lí kāi	ㄌㄧˊ ㄎㄞ	離開	leave	离开	L7

lì shǐ	ㄌㄧˋ ㄕˇ	歷史*	history	历史	L4
liáo tiān	ㄌㄧㄠˊ ㄊㄧㄢ	聊天*	chat		L8
liú	ㄌㄧㄡˊ	留	stay		L9
liú huà	ㄌㄧㄡˊ ㄏㄨㄚˋ	留話	leave a message	留话	L8
liù gǒu	ㄌㄧㄡˋ ㄍㄡˇ	遛狗*	walk the dog		L6
lóng	ㄌㄨㄥˊ	龍	dragon	龙	L5
lóng yǎn	ㄌㄨㄥˊ ㄧㄢˇ	龍眼	longan	龙眼	L5
M					
má pó dòu fu	ㄇㄚˊ ㄆㄛˊ ㄉㄡˋ ˙ㄈㄨ	麻婆豆腐	Mapo Tofu		L5
màn huà shū	ㄇㄢˋ ㄏㄨㄚˋ ㄕㄨ	漫畫書*	comic book	漫画书	L4
měi guó	ㄇㄟˇ ㄍㄨㄛˊ	美國	the U.S.	美国	L2
měi guó rén	ㄇㄟˇ ㄍㄨㄛˊ ㄖㄣˊ	美國人	American	美国人	L1
měi hǎo	ㄇㄟˇ ㄏㄠˇ	美好*	fine		L1
mì	ㄇㄧˋ	糸*	(a Chinese radical meaning silk)	纟	L10
mián	ㄇㄧㄢˊ	宀*	(a Chinese radical meaning roof or house)		L10
mó hú	ㄇㄛˊ ㄏㄨˊ	模糊*	confused	模糊	L10
mò xī gē	ㄇㄛˋ ㄒㄧ ㄍㄜ	墨西哥*	Mexico		L2
mù	ㄇㄨˋ	木*	(a Chinese radical meaning wood)		L10
N					
nà yàng	ㄋㄚˋ ㄧㄤˋ	那樣	in that way	那样	L1
nán fēi	ㄋㄢˊ ㄈㄟ	南非*	South Africa		L2
nán hái	ㄋㄢˊ ㄏㄞˊ	男孩	boy		L3*/L6
nán hái zi	ㄋㄢˊ ㄏㄞˊ ˙ㄗ	男孩子	boy		L6
nán shēng	ㄋㄢˊ ㄕㄥ	男生	male		L2
nán xìng	ㄋㄢˊ ㄒㄧㄥˋ	男性*	male		L3
nǎo	ㄋㄠˇ	腦	brain	脑	L10
ne	˙ㄋㄜ	呢	(interrogative tag used at the end of a question)		L6
nèi xiàng	ㄋㄟˋ ㄒㄧㄤˋ	內向	introverted	内向	L3
nǐ	ㄋㄧˇ	妳	you (feminine)		L3

nián gāo	ㄋㄧㄢˊ ㄍㄠ	年糕	glutinous rice cake		L9
nián jí	ㄋㄧㄢˊ ㄐㄧˊ	年级	grade	年级	L2
nián nián yǒu yú	ㄋㄧㄢˊ ㄋㄧㄢˊ ㄧㄡˇ ㄩˊ	年年有餘*	may there be surpluses every year	年年有余	L9
nián yè fàn	ㄋㄧㄢˊ ㄧㄝˋ ㄈㄢˋ	年夜飯	reunion dinner	年夜饭	L9
niàn	ㄋㄧㄢˋ	念	read out		L4
niǔ xī lán	ㄋㄧㄡˇ ㄒㄧ ㄌㄢˊ	紐西蘭*	New Zealand	纽西兰	L2
nǚ hái	ㄋㄩˇ ㄏㄞˊ	女孩	girl		L3
nǚ rén	ㄋㄩˇ ㄖㄣˊ	女人	woman		L10
nǚ xìng	ㄋㄩˇ ㄒㄧㄥˋ	女性*	female		L3
P					
pà	ㄆㄚˋ	怕	frighten		L5
...pái	……ㄆㄞˊ	……排	row		L8
pái duì	ㄆㄞˊ ㄉㄨㄟˋ	排隊	queue up	排队	L8
pí dàn	ㄆㄧˊ ㄉㄢˋ	皮蛋	preserved egg; century egg		L5
piào liàng	ㄆㄧㄠˋ ㄌㄧㄤˋ	漂亮*	pretty	漂亮	L1
pǐn dé	ㄆㄧㄣˇ ㄉㄜˊ	品德*	moral character		L1
píng ān	ㄆㄧㄥˊ ㄢ	平安	safe		L1*/L9
pū chuáng	ㄆㄨ ㄔㄨㄤˊ	鋪床*	make the bed	铺床	L6
Q					
qí guài	ㄑㄧˊ ㄍㄨㄞˋ	奇怪	strange		L10
qí huàn	ㄑㄧˊ ㄏㄨㄢˋ	奇幻*	fantasy		L4
qí tā	ㄑㄧˊ ㄊㄚ	其他	other		L3
qiān	ㄑㄧㄢ	千	thousand		L5
qiē	ㄑㄧㄝ	切*	cut		L7
qiē cài bǎn	ㄑㄧㄝ ㄘㄞˋ ㄅㄢˇ	切菜板*	chopping block	切菜板	L7
qīng / qīng sè	ㄑㄧㄥ / ㄑㄧㄥ ㄙㄜˋ	青/青色	green		L10
qīng chǔ	ㄑㄧㄥ ㄔㄨˇ	清楚	clear; lucid		L10
qǔ (míng zi)	ㄑㄩˇ (ㄇㄧㄥˊ ˙ㄗ)	取(名字)	give a name		L1
què	ㄑㄩㄝˋ	卻	but	却	L4

R

ràng	ㄖㄤˋ	讓	allow; give way to	让	L1
rè shuǐ	ㄖㄜˋ ㄕㄨㄟˇ	熱水	hot water	热水	L7
rì běn	ㄖˋ ㄅㄣˇ	日本	Japan		L2
rì wén	ㄖˋ ㄨㄣˊ	日文	Japanese		L2
rì zi	ㄖˋ ·ㄗ	日子	day		L7
rú guǒ	ㄖㄨˊ ㄍㄨㄛˇ	如果	if		L1

S

sǎo dì	ㄙㄠˇ ㄉㄧˋ	掃地*	sweep the floor	扫地	L6
sǐ	ㄙˇ	死	die		L1
suān	ㄙㄨㄢ	酸*	sour		L5
suī rán	ㄙㄨㄟ ㄖㄢˊ	雖然	although	虽然	L6
suì suì píng ān	ㄙㄨㄟˋ ㄙㄨㄟˋ ㄆㄧㄥˊ ㄢ	歲歲平安*	may you be safe through the years	岁岁平安	L9
shā wū dì ā lā bó	ㄕㄚ ㄨ ㄉㄧˋ ㄚ ㄌㄚ ㄅㄛˊ	沙烏地阿拉伯*	Saudi Arabia	沙乌地阿拉伯	L2
shài yī fú	ㄕㄞˋ ㄧ ㄈㄨˊ	曬衣服*	hang the laundry in the sun	晒衣服	L6
shāng diàn	ㄕㄤ ㄉㄧㄢˋ	商店	store		L8
shén huà	ㄕㄣˊ ㄏㄨㄚˋ	神話*	myth	神话	L4
shēng	ㄕㄥ	生*	born		L1
shēng yīn	ㄕㄥ ㄧㄣ	聲音	sound	声音	L9
shí	ㄕˊ	食*	(a Chinese radical meaning eating or food)		L10
shī	ㄕ	詩	poetry	诗	L4
shī huǒ	ㄕ ㄏㄨㄛˇ	失火*	catch fire		L7
shí wàn	ㄕˊ ㄨㄢˋ	十萬	one hundred thousand	十万	L4
shōu	ㄕㄡ	收	keep; tidy		L6
shōu shí wǎn pán	ㄕㄡ ㄕˊ ㄨㄢˇ ㄆㄢˊ	收拾碗盤*	clear the dishes	收拾碗盘	L6
shòu shāng	ㄕㄡˋ ㄕㄤ	受傷*	injured	受伤	L7
shū míng	ㄕㄨ ㄇㄧㄥˊ	書名*	title	书名	L4
shuā mǎ tǒng	ㄕㄨㄚ ㄇㄚˇ ㄊㄨㄥˇ	刷馬桶*	scrub the toilet bowl	刷马桶	L6
shuǐ guǒ	ㄕㄨㄟˇ ㄍㄨㄛˇ	水果	fruit		L5
shuǐ hú	ㄕㄨㄟˇ ㄏㄨˊ	水壺*	kettle	水壶	L7
shuǐ jiǎo	ㄕㄨㄟˇ ㄐㄧㄠˇ	水餃	dumpling	水饺	L9

shuǐ lóng tóu	ㄕㄨㄟˇ ㄌㄨㄥˊ ㄊㄡˊ	水龍頭*	tap	水龙头	L7
shùn lì	ㄕㄨㄣˋ ㄌㄧˋ	順利*	smooth-sailing	顺利	L1
shuō huà	ㄕㄨㄛ ㄏㄨㄚˋ	說話	talk	说话	L3

T

tái wān	ㄊㄞˊ ㄨㄢ	臺灣	Taiwan	台湾	L2
táng	ㄊㄤˊ	糖*	sugar		L5
tàng shāng	ㄊㄤˋ ㄕㄤ	燙傷*	scald	烫伤	L7
tàng yī fú	ㄊㄤˋ ㄧ ㄈㄨˊ	燙衣服*	iron the laundry	烫衣服	L6
tǐ tiē	ㄊㄧˇ ㄊㄧㄝ	體貼*	considerate	体贴	L3
tián	ㄊㄧㄢˊ	甜	sweet		L5*/L9
tiē	ㄊㄧㄝ	貼	paste	贴	L8
tóng huà	ㄊㄨㄥˊ ㄏㄨㄚˋ	童話*	children's stories; fairy tales	童话	L4
tóu	ㄊㄡˊ	頭	head	头	L5
tú huà shū	ㄊㄨˊ ㄏㄨㄚˋ ㄕㄨ	圖畫書*	picture book	图画书	L4
tuī lǐ	ㄊㄨㄟ ㄌㄧˇ	推理*	logic and reason		L4
tuō dì	ㄊㄨㄛ ㄌㄧˋ	拖地*	mop the floor		L6

W

wǎ sī lú	ㄨㄚˇ ㄙ ㄌㄨˊ	瓦斯爐*	gas stove	瓦斯炉	L7
wài xiàng	ㄨㄞˋ ㄒㄧㄤˋ	外向	extroverted		L3
wàn shì rú yì	ㄨㄢˋ ㄕˋ ㄖㄨˊ ㄧˋ	萬事如意*	may all of your wishes come true	万事如意	L9
wàng jì	ㄨㄤˋ ㄐㄧˋ	忘記*	forget	忘记	L1
wéi bō lú	ㄨㄟˊ ㄅㄛ ㄌㄨˊ	微波爐*	microwave oven	微波炉	L7
wéi xiǎn	ㄨㄟˊ ㄒㄧㄢˇ	危險*	dangerous	危险	L7
wèi le	ㄨㄟˋ ˙ㄌㄜ	為了	in order to; because of	为了	L1
wēn hé	ㄨㄣ ㄏㄜˊ	溫和*	mild	温和	L3
wēn róu	ㄨㄣ ㄖㄡˊ	溫柔*	culture	温柔	L3
wén huà	ㄨㄣˊ ㄏㄨㄚˋ	文化	gentle		L3
wǔ fàn	ㄨˇ ㄈㄢˋ	午飯	lunch	午饭	L8
wǔ xiá	ㄨˇ ㄒㄧㄚˊ	武俠*	sword-fighting	武侠	L4

X

xī bān yá	ㄒㄧ ㄅㄢ ㄧㄚˊ	西班牙*	Spain		L2
xī dì	ㄒㄧ ㄌㄧˋ	吸地*	vacuum the floor		L6

Pinyin	Zhuyin	Traditional	English	Simplified	Lesson
xǐ chuāng lián	ㄒㄧˇ ㄔㄨㄤ ㄌㄧㄢˊ	洗窗簾*	wash the curtains	洗窗帘	L6
xǐ yī diàn	ㄒㄧˇ ㄧ ㄉㄧㄢˋ	洗衣店	Laundromat		L3
xǐ yù gāng	ㄒㄧˇ ㄩˋ ㄍㄤ	洗浴缸*	wash the bath tub	洗浴缸	L6
xián	ㄒㄧㄢˊ	鹹*	salty	咸	L5
xiāng gǎng	ㄒㄧㄤ ㄍㄤˇ	香港*	Hong Kong		L2
xiàng	ㄒㄧㄤˋ	像	like; alike		L1
xiǎo hái	ㄒㄧㄠˇ ㄏㄞˊ	小孩	child		L6
xiǎo shí hòu	ㄒㄧㄠˇ ㄕˊ ㄏㄡˋ	小時候	when one was younger	小时候	L4
xiǎo shuō	ㄒㄧㄠˇ ㄕㄨㄛ	小說	novel	小说	L4
xiǎo xué	ㄒㄧㄠˇ ㄒㄩㄝˊ	小學	elementary school	小学	L2
xiào chē	ㄒㄧㄠˋ ㄔㄜ	校車*	school bus	校车	L8
xiào yuán	ㄒㄧㄠˋ ㄩㄢˊ	校園	campus	校园	L8
xié zi	ㄒㄧㄝˊ ˙ㄗ	鞋子	shoe		L8
xīn nián	ㄒㄧㄣ ㄋㄧㄢˊ	新年	New Year		L9
xīn xiǎng shì chéng	ㄒㄧㄣ ㄒㄧㄤˇ ㄕˋ ㄔㄥˊ	心想事成*	may all of your desires be fulfilled		L9
xìng bié	ㄒㄧㄥˋ ㄅㄧㄝˊ	性別*	gender	性别	L3
xiōng dì	ㄒㄩㄥ ㄉㄧˋ	兄弟*	brothers		L1

Y

Pinyin	Zhuyin	Traditional	English	Simplified	Lesson
yā / yā zhe	ㄧㄚ / ㄧㄚ˙ㄓㄜ	壓/壓著	pressed down; suppress	压/压着	L9
yā suì qián	ㄧㄚ ㄙㄨㄟˋ ㄑㄧㄢˊ	壓歲錢	money given to children during the Lunar New Year	压岁钱	L9
yán	ㄧㄢˊ	鹽*	salt	盐	L5
yán	ㄧㄢˊ	言*	(a Chinese radical meaning speech)		L10
yǎn	ㄧㄢˇ	广*	(a Chinese radical meaning houses on the cliff)		L10
yáo tóu / yáo yáo tóu	ㄧㄠˊ ㄊㄡˊ / ㄧㄠˊ ㄧㄠˊ ㄊㄡˊ	搖頭/搖搖頭	shake head	摇头/摇摇头	L5
yí dìng	ㄧˊ ㄉㄧㄥˋ	一定	definitely		L6
yǐ hòu	ㄧˇ ㄏㄡˋ	以後	after; later	以后	L3
yǐ jīng	ㄧˇ ㄐㄧㄥ	已經	already	已经	L6
yì dà lì	ㄧˋ ㄉㄚˋ ㄌㄧˋ	義大利*	Italy	意大利	L2

yì fán fēng shùn	ㄧˋ ㄈㄢˊ ㄈㄥ ㄕㄨㄣˋ	一帆風順*	may everything go smoothly for you	一帆风顺	L9
yì si	ㄧˋ ·ㄙ	意思	meaning		L1
yì xiē	ㄧˋ ㄒㄧㄝ	一些	some		L3
yì zhě	ㄧˋ ㄓㄜˇ	譯者*	translator	译者	L4
yìn dù	ㄧㄣˋ ㄉㄨˋ	印度	India		L2
yīng gāi	ㄧㄥ ㄍㄞ	應該	should	应该	L10
yīng guó	ㄧㄥ ㄍㄨㄛˊ	英國	the U.K.	英国	L2
yīng guó rén	ㄧㄥ ㄍㄨㄛˊ ㄖㄣˊ	英國人	British	英国人	L2
yōu mò	ㄧㄡ ㄇㄛˋ	幽默*	humorous		L3
yóu	ㄧㄡˊ	油*	oil		L5
yǒu míng	ㄧㄡˇ ㄇㄧㄥˊ	有名	well-known		L5
yú	ㄩˊ	餘	excess	余	L9
yú shì	ㄩˊ ㄕˋ	於是	so; then	于是	L5
yù yán	ㄩˋ ㄧㄢˊ	寓言*	fable		L4
yuán lái	ㄩㄢˊ ㄌㄞˊ	原來	original	原来	L2
yuàn yì	ㄩㄢˋ ㄧˋ	願意	willing	愿意	L8
yuàn zi	ㄩㄢˋ ·ㄗ	院子	courtyard		L6
yuè	ㄩㄝˋ	越	more		L4
yuè nán	ㄩㄝˋ ㄋㄢˊ	越南	Vietnam		L3
yuè nán rén	ㄩㄝˋ ㄋㄢˊ ㄖㄣˊ	越南人	Vietnamese		L3
yùn qì	ㄩㄣˋ ㄑㄧˋ	運氣	luck	运气	L2

Z

zá zhì	ㄗㄚˊ ㄓˋ	雜誌*	magazine	杂志	L4
zì xìn	ㄗˋ ㄒㄧㄣˋ	自信*	confident		L3
zǒu láng	ㄗㄡˇ ㄌㄤˊ	走廊*	corridor		L8
zuì hòu	ㄗㄨㄟˋ ㄏㄡˋ	最後	finally	最后	L1
zuò zhě	ㄗㄨㄛˋ ㄓㄜˇ	作者*	author		L4
zhá	ㄓㄚˊ	炸*	deep-fry		L7
zhàn	ㄓㄢˋ	站	stand		L10
zhǎng dà	ㄓㄤˇ ㄉㄚˋ	長大	grow up	长大	L2
zhāo cái jìn bǎo	ㄓㄠ ㄘㄞˊ ㄐㄧㄣˋ ㄅㄠˇ	招財進寶*	may you bring in wealth and fortune	招财进宝	L9
zhé yī fú	ㄓㄜˊ ㄧ ㄈㄨˊ	摺衣服*	fold the laundry	折衣服	L6

zhè xiē	ㄓㄜˋ ㄒㄧㄝ	這些	these	这些	L4
zhēng	ㄓㄥ	蒸	steam	蒸	L7
zhēng chǎo	ㄓㄥ ㄔㄠˇ	爭吵	quarrel	争吵	L10
zhěng lǐ	ㄓㄥˇ ㄌㄧˇ	整理	tidy up		L6
zhèng cháng	ㄓㄥˋ ㄔㄤˊ	正常*	normal		L10
zhì lì	ㄓˋ ㄌㄧˋ	智利*	Chile		L2
zhōng guó	ㄓㄨㄥ ㄍㄨㄛˊ	中國	China	中国	L2
zhōng huá	ㄓㄨㄥ ㄏㄨㄚˊ	中華	Chinese	中华	L3
zhōng xué	ㄓㄨㄥ ㄒㄩㄝˊ	中學	secondary school	中学	L2
zhōng xué shēng	ㄓㄨㄥ ㄒㄩㄝˊ ㄕㄥ	中學生	secondary school student	中学生	L2
zhú	ㄓㄨˊ	竹*	(a Chinese radical meaning bamboo)		L10
zhǔ	ㄓㄨˇ	煮*	cook		L7
zhǔ dòng	ㄓㄨˇ ㄉㄨㄥˋ	主動*	take initiative	主动	L3